JAMES CONE IN PLAIN ENGLISH

STEPHEN D. MORRISON

BELOVED PUBLISHING • COLUMBUS, OHIO

Print ISBN: 978-1-63174-177-7

eBook ISBN: 978-1-63174-178-4

Beloved Publishing · Columbus, Ohio.

Acknowledgements:

I want to thank Dr. William Reese, Jr., for his valuable encouragement and feedback.

As always, I am deeply indebted to my beloved wife, Ketlin. Your support means everything to me.

This book is dedicated to the victims of white supremacy.

CONTENTS

INTRODUCTION

One of the reasons it is so hard to talk about race is that we don't think we have to. And for white people, that may be true. We do not have to talk about race because our whiteness has been deemed "normal" and "beautiful" by society. White privilege affords the illusion of not "seeing color." But black people around the world have never had that luxury. White supremacy violently oppresses black and brown bodies every day. The idea that we live in a post-racial society is a ploy to ease the guilty conscience of white people. It is a myth. We must talk about race because we do not live in a just world—*because a better world is possible.*

This is a hard book. It was hard to write, and it will probably be hard to read. That is not necessarily because the ideas presented here are difficult to grasp, but because they require something from us, something more than mere intellectual agreement. James Cone's theology is not the kind we can read casually. To read James Cone is to be forcefully awakened from our slumber and repent of our apathy.

I almost called this book *James Cone for White People*. It would not have been an inaccurate title. Even though my primary aim is to explain the major ideas in Cone's theology, I cannot escape myself. I am white. And Cone's work forcefully disrupts the comfortable illusions of white people like me. He did not write theology for me; he wrote for the sake of black liberation. And in that struggle, I am the natural oppressor. Thus, black liberation demands the destruction of white illusions. If we hold too tightly to an unreal image of ourselves, we will reject the truth because it threatens our idealized identity. The truth will set you free, but first, it will hurt. Just as daylight stings the eyes of a man stumbling out of a cave for the first time, the truth is often painful. Still, we must repent and see ourselves rightly through the experiences of the poor and oppressed.

This book may be a difficult pill to swallow, but above all else, it will be honest. That is my only promise. And in my limited way, I hope to convince you that James Cone was right—right about so many things, but firstly, he was right that the Church and theology must become antiracist for Christ's sake.

Racism and theology

To live in a world of white supremacy means we must take sides. Neutrality is an illusion that only helps the oppressor. Cone calls us to forgo the false comfort of color-blindness and embrace a new vision of the world, to become antiracists. There is no middle ground in the struggle for justice. We are either racists or antiracists; either we stand by in complicit silence, hiding behind the illusion of color-blindness, or take up the fight against oppression.

James Cone's work is a prophetic call for the Church to return to the Gospel of liberation. In the same way that Barth's *Der Römerbrief* went off like a bombshell in the theologian's playground,[1] so Christian theology is at a watershed moment with the work of James Cone. He shatters the illusion of doing theology without acting on the political imperatives of Christ's Gospel, i.e., theology without praxis. Cone forces us to confront the reality that theology has more often been an ally to white supremacy than a threat to it. For too long, theologians have hidden away in an ivory tower of academic objectivism. We have ignored racism, and by ignoring it, we have been complicit in its injustices. But silence in the face of evil is sinful.

My perspective has been radically disrupted by reading James Cone. This is now the fifth book in my "Plain English" series. For the first American theologian of the series, I wanted to honor the man I consider to be the most significant voice in American theology today. He wrestled with such a uniquely (though not exclusively) American problem like no theologian before him. Racism is undoubtedly America's original, founding sin, second perhaps only to its greed. Yet American theology has altogether ignored it as a theological problem.

Accordingly, I hope to show that James Cone is America's greatest theologian. Or, if not *the* greatest, certainly among the most significant. While the question is often a moot point—an exercise that reveals more about personal bias than the theologians themselves—it reveals our priorities. The two names most commonly considered for the title are Jonathan Edwards and Charles Hodge. But both Edwards and Hodge owned slaves for the majority of their lives. Their theological merits still matter, of course, but what about the ethical implications of their theology? Can a theology that permits owning another human be the "greatest" America ever produced? Can a theologian be the "cream of the crop" if their work altogether ignores the greatest sin America has committed and commits still to this day?

James Cone considered Martin Luther King, Jr., America's greatest theologian. But while King accomplished much for the liberation of oppressed black men and women in America, it was without significantly changing the way theologians confront racism. Therefore, just about everyone today embraces King as a prophetic civil rights leader, but few take his work as a challenge to theology itself. Theologians continue on their merry way, praising King yet remaining faithful to a theology that either actively cultivates racism or fails to confront it head-on (which, in the end, is the same thing). So while King may rightly be America's most celebrated activist, he did not wrestle theologically with racism enough to be considered America's greatest theologian.

On the other hand, James Cone endeavored to dismantle the structures that normalize Christian racism theologically. And those structures are more ingrained in our thinking than we would like to admit. Cone's genius is the realization that racism is a theological problem, and until we confront it as such, theology and the Church will continue as if it has nothing to say about the systemic oppression of the poor, black, foreign, and marginalized. Until the plight of the oppressed becomes a central theological theme (as it is in Scripture), theology will remain complicit in oppression because of its silence. As Fredrick Herzog warns, "If we do not turn our theological attention to the oppressed we will never understand the Gospel."[2]

Faith without works is dead. So theology without revolutionary praxis is little more than a lifeless ideology. Theology cannot ignore its political imperatives in favor of idle, speculative language games. Any theology that fails to challenge the status quo is not worthy of the name of the One who stands in unwavering solidarity with the poor and helpless. The cross is the shattering point where theology becomes either a dead, pointless game or a revolutionary call to change the world.

Liberation theology in general, and black theology in particular, takes Marx's famous eleventh thesis on Feuerbach seriously: "Philosophers have hitherto only *interpreted* the world in various ways; the point is to *change* it."[3] Cone's work rejects any theology that does not lead to political praxis. Theology has real-world implications. The point is not merely to interpret the Bible or to understand God abstractly, but rather, it is to join God in the fight to liberate the oppressed; bring good news to the poor; proclaim release to the captives, sight to the blind, and announce the year of the Lord's favor. The Church of Jesus Christ must be antiracist, taking sides against white supremacy in the name of God.

Personal reflections

I am a white, middle-class, heterosexual, cis-gendered male. I am privileged in all realms of life: socially, politically, and economically. In every sense, I am the oppressor, and I cannot shy away from this fact. I am racist because I am a white man living in a racist system from which I benefit significantly. And I have not only inherited a racist system but also internalized its impulses and judgments. I am not innocent.

While there are substantial differences between personal and systemic racism, I cannot claim to be free from either. No honest white person can or should try to uphold such an idealistic image of themselves. It is an illusion. According to 1 John 1:8, "If we say that we have no sin, we deceive ourselves, and the truth is not in us."[4] We must repent of our illusions of racial innocence. Just as no individual can claim sinlessness, no white person can claim to be innocent of white supremacy. I may argue that I do everything I can to avoid being racist personally, but I cannot excuse myself from the racist systems of this world that privilege me because of my skin tone. I have benefited from racism all my life. Every white person has.

So this is my confession: I am and have been racist. *No white person can claim anything less.* To be white is to benefit from a system of white supremacy. I cannot guarantee that I am free from racist impulses because I have read and now written about James Cone. The environment in which I live has taught me to accept certain prejudices that are not quickly abandoned. But I am slowly becoming more aware of my impulses, and I am learning a new way of being human. In other words, I am repenting—*daily, hourly.* Repentance is not a one-and-done transaction; it is a lifelong journey. Reading James Cone is only the beginning, and I hope to share this journey with you. I pray this book will help other white people like me recognize their privilege and take up the antiracist mandate.

But it is not only on a personal level that we must repent. As a society, we must fight to dismantle the racist policies that keep white supremacy in place. Racism is a personal issue, but it is also a political one. The systemic policies of racism do more to enforce white supremacy than the acts of individual racists. And as Ibram X. Kendi has powerfully shown, the former often establishes the latter.[5] To be antiracist is to be politically concerned with every policy that has racist results, no matter the original, nominal intentions. We must repent of our racist impulses, but we must also fight to dismantle the political policies that support white supremacy. Racism is neither a purely personal or political issue; it is both.

We never talked about racism in the Church of my youth. I can only recall one mixed family who regularly attended service; my Church was overwhelmingly white. Racism was not a subject we discussed. It is not that we were apolitical. We talked about political issues quite often, but it was only the kinds of issues that mattered to whiteness. These included abortion, gay marriage, the military, and terrorism, but it never included systemic racism, the war on drugs, or the prison-industrial complex. My pastor would often go on political rants about Obama after he was elected to office, rarely having a positive thing to say. On Veterans Day and Memorial Day, we would march in a patriotic parade through the Church while singing The Battle Hymn of the Republic. Nationalism was perfectly acceptable, but we never discussed racism or the plight of the oppressed. We praised America the beautiful and free but turned our eyes away from America the enslaver, oppressor, imperialist, and racist. It is a sure sign of white privilege when we get to pick and choose what to be angry about. In a racist society that statistically discriminates against black men and women, to say nothing about race is the epitome of white privilege. But it is also what I would now call sin.

That is why the prophetic voice of James Cone is of unparalleled importance in the Church today. I grew up never hearing about the sin of white supremacy because I was complicit in its grievances; I never heard a single sermon about the sin of racism because I benefited from racism. James Cone confronts the Church with the hard truth of our rampant sin.

But the truth will set us free. I would rather live in the hard light of reality than in the comfortable illusion of falsity. Cone has helped me see my privilege. Most importantly, he has helped me realize that renouncing my privileged status to take up solidarity with the oppressed is a Christian obligation. To be a Christian means to follow Jesus Christ, who was unequivocally on the side of the underclass. The discipleship of Christ means following the road Christ walked, of which Paul writes, "[He] emptied himself, taking the form of a slave [. . .] He humbled himself and became obedient to the point of death—even death on the cross" (Philippians 2:7-8). The way of Christ is the way of death, the death of the old, privileged, elitist self. In the words of what is perhaps Cone's most difficult metaphor, we must renounce whiteness, be born again, and "become black" with Christ in solidarity with the oppressed.

What can someone with my privileges offer in the fight for liberation? That is not an easy question, but it has haunted me ever since I began this journey. For a few years now, I have been reading Cone's work alongside other liberation theologians such as Boff, Gutiérrez, Soelle, and Ruether. They have opened my eyes to new theological possibilities that feel fresh and exciting, but they have also been extremely challenging. The journey has led me to adopt a clear vision of what theology should say to a world of racism, sexism, and capitalist exploitation. But it has also forced me to become more self-aware and self-critical of my position in society.

Thus, for a long time, I wrestled with the feeling that writing this book would be inappropriate. I felt like I would only hurt the cause of black liberation by adding another ignorant white voice to the conversation. I thought it might be best if I remained silent. Perhaps that is still true. But every time I wanted to forgo this book because of my fears, I felt that I *must* say something. I may be white and privileged, but I can use my voice to fight against oppression. And through my journey, perhaps I can call out to my fellow white, privileged Christians, and show them just how much we have missed the Gospel with our theological language games. And this is what I intend to do.[6] Cone's black theology is not for me; in many ways, it is *against* me. But it is against me in the same way that the Gospel is against me, by calling me to repentance. It is a scandal and an offense, but it is truth. And thus, it is freedom.

So I prayerfully and humbly submit this book to support the cause of black liberation in the world today by shining a light on Cone's work. I cannot control how it will be received. But at the end of the day, I would not be true to myself if I did not say something. As a theologian, I believe that by placing James Cone's contributions in equal esteem with the works of Barth, Schleiermacher, and the others in this series, I can help highlight just how important he is for theology today. Cone's work is no less significant than theirs. If any theologian deserves a library of books about them, it is James Cone. Students who study Barth, Bultmann, and Tillich at university should also read Cone—for the future of the Church and the world.

We are in the middle of a rapidly changing society. Racism and fascism are on the rise. The Church will either be complicit in the unjust exploitation of the underprivileged or stand up and fight against the evils of racism and oppression. I hope that anyone reading this book will be convinced of the truth of Cone's major claims and then put it down with a life-long commitment to the cause of liberation worldwide. This does not mean that we cannot or should not critically engage with Cone or disagree with him at times, but I hope the days of altogether ignoring him will quickly come to an end. His prophetic voice is far too vital.

Cone's work calls the Church to renounce its privileged status and embrace the discipleship of Christ. Indeed, it is only in the midst of the least of these that Christ is present. God is with the needy, poor, homeless, and black. It is time for the Church to live in the fellowship of Christ and not the courts of Herod.

Systemic racism

White privilege and systemic racism are two of the most contentious issues in discussions about race. I want to take the time to unpack these terms because they will be vital for understanding James Cone and his theology.

I would define systemic racism as the political policies, economic institutions, and social structures that uphold white supremacy by oppressing non-whites and distributing the power, resources, and opportunities in society to white people. "Institutional racism" was coined by Stokely Carmichael (Kwame Ture) and Charles V. Hamilton. Their definition remains one of the best for clarifying the distinctions between personal and systemic racism, so I quote it at length:

> By 'racism' we mean the predication of decisions and policies on considerations of race for the purpose of *subordinating* a racial group and maintaining control over that group. [...] Racism is both overt and covert. It takes two, closely related forms: individual whites acting

against individual blacks, and acts by the total white community against the black community. We call these individual racism and institutional racism. [...] When white terrorists bomb a black church and kill five black children, that is an act of individual racism, widely deplored by most segments of the society. But when in that same city—Birmingham, Alabama—five hundred black babies die each year because of the lack of proper food, shelter and medical facilities, and thousands more are destroyed and maimed physically, emotionally, and intellectually because of conditions of poverty and discrimination in the black community, that is a function of institutional racism. [...] 'Respectable' individuals can absolve themselves from blame; *they* would never plant a bomb in a church; *they* would never stone a black family. But they continue to support political officials and institutions that would and do perpetuate institutionally racist policies. Thus *acts* of overt, individual racism may not typify the society, but institutional racism does—with the support of covert, individual *attitudes* of racism.[7]

Racism is not primarily about the overtly racist acts of white suprema-cists. It is about the political policies which organize and structure society. Systemic racism, then, is the prevalence of policies that oppress persons of color. People are racist when they do racist things, but it is primarily by supporting racist policies that racism is systemically established as the norm. Individuals may try to excuse themselves from racism personally, but if they support racist policies, they are promoting racism, whether they realize it or not.

A white person born into a white supremacist society cannot *not* be racist because they unavoidably benefit from racist policies. That is why I said I am and have been racist. I was born white and am guilty of white supremacy. It is an inherited sin. Whenever a white person silently accepts the racist norm, they are guilty of upholding white supremacy. Personal and systemic racism are interconnected, with the latter often informing and establishing the former, and so we must expand our definition of racism to include both.

This interplay explains why Cone concluded that no white person in the world today can feign racial innocence; to be white is to be guilty of white supremacy irrespective of personal actions. It is what he calls "whiteness." A white person is born into a world that benefits them signif-icantly by offering them better advantages and opportunities because of their skin color. But what a white person chooses to do with their privilege, whether they acclimate to whiteness or fight against it, makes all the difference; we can either be racist by our silence or antiracist by working to overthrow white supremacy. There is no third option.

So the question becomes: What is a racist policy? A policy is deemed racist not according to its intended outcome but by its actual results. For example: the war on drugs is arguably the most racist modern policy in America, especially if we include its offspring, the prison-industrial complex. Drug crimes are enforced more harshly on black people than white people, leading to a sizable statistical disparity in America's bloated prison population, even though white people are just as likely to commit the same crimes.[8] Furthermore, white drug offenders are often met with leniency, while black offenders guilty of the same crimes are punished harshly.[9] Whatever the initial aim was for the war on drugs, and despite its claim to color-blindness, it is verifiably racist.

Racist policies such as these then reinforce racist stereotypes on a personal and social level by creating the conditions for them. When more black men are criminalized for drug use, black people are stereotyped as drug addicts, black families as broken, black fathers as absent, and black neighborhoods as dangerous ghettos. But these are all *symptoms* of a policy that systemically discriminates against black people. In this sense, racist policies are like self-fulfilling prophecies; the policy creates the circumstances that then re-enforce and verify racist stereotypes with statistics, but these stereotypes would not exist if it were not for the racist policy. This same cycle surrounds every racist policy, such as those tax policies which systemically rob adequate funding from schools in black neighborhoods. That policy reinforces the stereotype of the lazy, under-performing black student by creating the circumstances necessary for that outcome by denying black schools the funds they need to provide quality education. If black students struggle to meet the same standards of white students, it is not because black students have failed to learn. Rather, it is because our society has altogether failed black students.

Systemic racism is a collection of policies that reinforce and often create personal biases and social stereotypes; in other words, racist policies give birth to racist ideas. Racist ideas verify themselves by the results of racist policies. It is a vicious cycle. It is a pattern that will be broken only by abolishing racist policies. That is what we must focus our attention on changing if we want to be antiracist. Personal prejudices are, of course, a problem, but the more significant issue is always the policies that reinforce and often create those biases. The history of segregation is a great example. Before the policy changed, most Americans were *for* segregation; but after the policy changed, a few years later, the majority of white people were *against* segregation.[10] When the policy changes, the racist idea it produced will have no ground to stand on.

One racist policy does not necessarily result in systemic racism. But there is not just one such policy in America; there are many. Black people can face discriminatory policies in nearly every aspect of their lives, from housing, employment, banking, law enforcement, incarceration, health care, social services, and education. But they also face the prejudicial biases and expectations of society, which limits black success, health, wellness, and wealth by denying the same advantages and opportunities white people receive by default. These expectations are often the result of the stereotypes originally created by racist policies. Systemic racism is a massively convoluted trap designed to keep black people in bondage and white people in power.

White privilege

Cone asks, "Could white people ever be made to truly understand the price blacks paid for their privilege?"[11] White privilege is the benefit white people are born with because of systemic racism—because black people are and have been oppressed for centuries. A white supremacist society provides better opportunities and fewer obstacles for white people to pursue success in life. In short, white privilege means white people get a head start.[12]

White privilege does *not* mean white people always have it better. Critics of the concept often point to examples of black success and white failure and use these to "prove" that white privilege is a myth. But that is to ignore the systemic policies that enforce white supremacy. The trick white supremacists use is to blame personal or moral failure instead of policy failure. When police kill unarmed black people at an alarming rate, white supremacy looks for what they did to "deserve" being lynched in the streets rather than asking why "law and order" policing means slaughtering black bodies with impunity. When black people are incarcerated five times more frequently than their white counterparts,[13] we ask why they commit more crimes (they don't) rather than why black people are arrested and punished more often for crimes white people are just as likely to commit. White privilege does not mean that life will always be easier for white people, but if and when it is hard, it is *not* because of the color of their skin.

Because of racist housing policies that confine black people to ghettoes and their children to poorly funded schools, white privilege means growing up in a "nicer" neighborhood with better schools and thus more opportunities for educational success. It also means that because of the racist idea these policies produced—namely, that black students do worse in school—teachers and educators often treat white students with more patience and care.[14] By assuming that black students will perform worse than their white counterparts, teachers fail to give them the same attention white students receive. There is a drastic difference between a student who is believed in by their teachers and a student deemed a lost cause from the start.[15]

White privilege is also, as I have mentioned, the privilege of imagining we are in a post-racial world. There is perhaps no idea more dangerous than the belief that we are beyond racism. The overt racism of a Klan member is, of course, a problem, but they are at least honest about their intentions. Whereas a white, privileged housewife can call the cops on a group of black people for gathering in a public park and still claim that she does not "see color."

Finally, white privilege means you are free to disregard everything I am saying here, to ignore the work of James Cone, write him off as a heretic—as so many white theologians do—and continue living life and doing theology as if racism does not affect the Christian faith. But this is not a privilege extended to black men and women around the world who cannot escape the tyranny of white supremacy, who are regularly reminded of their status in society as second-class citizens, and who live with a daily struggle to assert the beauty of their blackness in a world that refuses to accept them as they are. Being white in such a world means renouncing our privilege and humbly listening to the stories of the black experience. Ultimately, it means supporting wholeheartedly the fight to end racial injustice on a systemic level.

To be antiracist requires constant self-awareness and self-criticism. It is hard work, but it is what Christ's Gospel commands from us. Racism is a sin from which we must repent. Personally and socially, we must repent of the racial biases we have adopted; we must acknowledge that we are not color-blind and begin the lifelong process of becoming antiracist. Politically, we must repent of racist policies and fight to overthrow them. Instead of focusing all our attention on personal prejudices, we must fight to dismantle the policies that uphold white supremacy. That is what it would look like for America to repent of its long history of racism. The same is true for theology. Cone calls the Church to repent of its uncritical allegiance to the power structures that uphold white supremacy. We are not innocent.

BIOGRAPHY

I was a theologian, asking: What, if anything, is theology worth in the
black struggle in America?[1]

— JAMES CONE

James Hal Cone was born on August 5, 1938, in Fordyce, Arkansas. He
grew up in the small town of Bearden, which he described as "a world
defined both by white supremacy and by the profound black spiritual
resistance it provoked."[2] This duality weighed heavily on his mind. If God
is all-powerful, loving, and good, why does God allow the systematic
oppression and mistreatment of black people?

Cone often cites the Bearden Macedonia African Methodist Episcopal
(AME) Church as a significant influence on his spiritual life. The freedom
and joy of their singing, the enthusiasm of their preaching, and their ever-
present spirit of liberation were vital developmental experiences, especially
as it stood in such stark contrast with the daily brutalities of white
supremacy. The effects of racism were not as overt as they could have
been, nor does Cone cite any particularly violent example of abuse. But a
culture of micro-aggressions made sure black people never forgot that they
were considered a lesser class of human. Various subtle but demeaning
societal norms reinforced the message of white supremacy. Cone recalls an
example. Whenever white people greeted each other it was respectful and

polite, calling one another "Mr." and "Mrs.," but whenever they greeted a black person, no matter their age, they were flippant and rude towards them by calling them "boy," "girl," or by their first name.

Cone's father refused to accept these dehumanizing norms. He always referred to his wife as "Mrs. Cone" in the presence of whites to deny them the option of using her first name, and he would not tolerate being called "boy." It may seem small, but his father's subtle act of protest established a strong sense of black dignity in Cone. Indeed, Cone reflects that his father's refusal to bow to whites' dehumanizing attempts sparked a bright flame of resentment in his heart against the injustices of white supremacy.

From his father, Cone discovered what it means never to sell your integrity. His father refused to let his mother work in white people's houses because of the near-certain risk of sexual harassment—even though they needed the money. They had to live in a world of white supremacy, but they did not have to acclimate to it. Cone writes, "The universal manifestation of courage and resistance that I saw in my father's life continues to make anything that I might achieve seem modest and sometimes insignificant."[3] Cone learned that black survival in an oppressive, white world required constant struggle. No one achieves liberation by staying in line and keeping quiet.

In such an oppressive environment, faith became the primary source of comfort and survival. Contrary to the Marxist critique of religion as the opium of oppressed people, Cone grew up with a keen awareness that his Christian faith disrupted the oppressive norms and inspired a powerful strength for resistance. No one is subhuman in the Church. Instead, within its four walls, he was a beloved child of God, a somebody rather than the nobody whites wanted him to be. As Cone writes, "The value structures in the society were completely reversed in the church."[4]

In 1954, Cone graduated high school and attended Shorter, a two-year unaccredited college of the AME Church. He later transferred to Philander Smith, a large, four-year accredited Methodist college in Little Rock. These schools opened up a new world, not only because Cone went from small-town life to the big city, but because it enlarged his perspective, particularly his understanding of how faith relates to justice. He began to read about Martin Luther King, Jr., and the Montgomery bus boycott, and he experienced firsthand the integration crisis of 1957. It did not take long for Cone to learn that white theology, despite all its lip-service to Christian values, was an immoral, anti-Christian ideology. No amount of clever theological justification could convince him that the whites who harassed the nine black children integrating into the largest white high school in Little Rock were Christians. The hypocrisy of white religion laid bare before his eyes in a new way.

One afternoon, Cone rode a public bus and experienced the contradictions of white Christianity directly. He decided to sit down next to a churchly-looking, elderly white lady. She quickly bolted up and began yelling curses at him. Cone calmly went over to her with a smile and said, "Madam, you look like a Christian, and that was why I sat down by you. How could you say the things you said to me when Jesus said that what you do to the least you do to him?" to which she replied violently, "You are not Jesus. Get the hell out of my face, you n——!"[5] From this experience and many others like it, Cone began to realize that there is a sharp divide between what people profess to believe and how they act in reality. For white Christianity, the gulf could not be more substantial. Cone realized: "Even if people know the truth, they will not necessarily do it […] religion did not automatically make people sensitive to human pain and suffering […] What white people needed was a conversion experience."[6] White Christianity, Cone discovered, is morally diseased and theologically deceived.

For Cone, the white Church's uncritical acceptance of white supremacy was as severe an offense, theologically speaking, as Catholic indulgences were to the Protestant Reformation. The failure to connect the Gospel to the plight of black people oppressed by white supremacy is a theological failure just as much as an ethical one. Racism is a heresy no less dangerous than Arianism.

In 1958, Cone left Little Rock for Evanston, Illinois, to attend Garrett Biblical Institute. What led Cone to pursue a major in religion and philosophy was his desire to "study the past in order to analyse the present, so that black people would know how to make a different future."[7] Cone's "ceaseless intellectual curiosity" was also driven by "the existential need to analyze the contradictions in the black experience."[8] But the change from a Southern to a Northern school was devastating, for both Cone and his brother, Cecil. It was a season of intellectual and emotional growth. Yet the devastation he felt stemmed most of all from his naïveté about the extra freedoms supposedly available to black people in the progressive North. It was a rude awakening to realize that white America was the same everywhere. The Northern states were no less racist; they were just better at hiding it.

One professor regularly and unashamedly told racist jokes in his classroom. Ironically, he taught Christian ethics. But he was also not an outlier. As Cone's professors informed him, the school did not expect black students to do any better than a C average. That infuriated Cone and drove him to work even harder, eventually working his way up to earning two Bs. By the time he was a senior, Cone was a straight-A student, passing his exams with distinction and even receiving a prize in systematic theology for excellence. It was also during his senior year that Cone decided to pursue a Ph.D. He was the first black candidate in Garrett's history. His academic advisor at the time said there was simply no way he would be accepted. But one of his professors, William Hordern —a valuable member of the faculty—courageously stood up for him: "Jim, you go right ahead and apply, and if you are not accepted, then I will quit."[9] Cone was accepted to the program, recalling fondly, "That was the first time that any white person ever put himself on the line for me."[10]

Pursuing a doctorate was an uphill battle, but it was not only because he faced such a severe academic bias. According to Cone, he struggled most of all under the sharp disparity between what he was learning in the classroom and the racial injustices taking place all around him. He remembers thinking, "How could I write papers about the Barth-Brunner debates on natural theology while black people were being denied the right to vote?"[11] This blindness gets to the heart of white theology's privileged academic elitism. In six years at Garrett, not a single required text was written by a black scholar, which had a profound effect on black students' self-esteem. But as Cone recalls, "Equally problematic for my stay at Garrett was the absence of the discussion of racism as a *theological* problem."[12] Cone found this "strange and racist." The white faculty did not think the Gospel had anything to do with racial oppression. White privilege deafened their ears to Christ crying out with the voice of the oppressed in their midst.

Ironically, Cone's professors refused to acknowledge racism as a theological problem even though the German-speaking theologians they studied with such reverence made the interdependence of theology, politics, and ethics central to their work. Bonhoeffer, Barth, Tillich, and Bultmann all considered Nazism a theological problem and resolutely stood against it, each in their way. Bonhoeffer was inspired by the black experience to resist Nazism after traveling to Harlem, visiting black churches, and witnessing their struggle against white supremacy firsthand.[13] But Cone's professors saw little to nothing wrong with the blatant racism and oppression in their backyard, even though they could see the theological importance of resisting Nazism and anti-Semitism on German soil. They were too blinded by their privilege to see that the black struggle for justice is also God's struggle.

Cone refused to ignore racism. In one particularly memorable class, he vehemently called his professor a racist because, while he could passionately talk about the injustices that Roman Catholics inflicted upon Protestants in the sixteenth century, he had nothing to say about the crime of white Christians brutally oppressing and dehumanizing black people today. The classroom fell silent, and his professor denied the charge. Cone quickly learned that he should avoid making the connection between theology and racism too explicit to his professors if he was going to survive Garrett and successfully earn his doctorate. That is why he completed his dissertation on Karl Barth's anthropology rather than an issue from the black community.

At graduation, Cone's ethics professor, who regularly told racist jokes, refused to shake his hand, skipping him to shake those of every other graduate (all of whom were white). But Cone was used to this by now and laughed about it to himself. What mattered was he accomplished what he set out to do, although he wasn't sure what to do next. He went back to teach at Philander Smith, wondering what Barth, Tillich, and Brunner had to do with the young black boys and girls from the fields of the South. Cone writes, "The contradiction between theology as a discipline and the struggle for black freedom in the streets was experienced at the deepest level of my being. [...] I had spent six years studying theology, and now I found it irrelevant to the things that mattered most to me."[14]

The tension developed further when, in 1964, Joseph Washington published *Black Religion*. Washington argued that black faith could not rightly be Christian faith because it identifies the Gospel with the struggle for justice in society. The Gospel, he explained, was about the doctrines of faith and creeds of the Church, not, as black faith held, about black justice and the civil rights movement. White theologians praised the book, while black theologians regarded it as poor scholarship and bad taste. Cone felt obligated to respond, and several preachers and teachers encouraged him to. Yet, he knew it would mean challenging the entire white theological establishment, a mammoth task he was not ready to take on. It would be another four years before he publicly spoke about a black theology of liberation.

In 1966, Cone left Philander Smith for a position at Adrian College, Michigan. It was here that an outline for black theology began to form more concretely in his mind, probably because Adrian provided him ample time to reflect on current events. As he became more involved in civil rights activism, Cone felt more and more that his theological training was altogether irrelevant to the struggle of black liberation. "How could I continue to allow my intellectual life to be consumed by the theological problems defined by people who had enslaved my grandparents?" He continues:

> I began to develop an intense dislike for theology because it avoided the really hard problems of life with its talk about revelation, God, Jesus, and the Holy Spirit. When the murderers of humanity seize control of the public meaning of the Christian faith, it is time to seek new ways of expressing the truth of the gospel.[15]

He could not teach white students about Barth and Tillich while black people were dying in the streets. Cone recalls how the 12th St., Detroit riot of July 1967 "woke me out of my academic world."[16] He felt a sense of urgency, "I had to do something."[17]

Cone's rage only grew as white theologians condemned the violence of black rioters while ignoring the police's more severe brutality. And most of all, he was angry that white theologians turned a blind eye to the violence of systemic racism that produced the riots in the first place. On what grounds did these white oppressors think they could teach the black oppressed about Christian ethics? How can white theology not see the hypocrisy of promoting peace with one hand while creating a system of violence against black people with the other? But that is how it works for those in power. They hide under the guise of law and order, peace, and nonviolence, yet they fail to acknowledge how the structures of society are guilty of violently oppressing the underprivileged classes. This tension led Cone to a new kind of writing, in which the "first priority was my black identity."[18] The result was a "brief manifesto identifying Black Power with the gospel of Jesus."[19] As he later reflected, "I had to find a *new* way of talking about God that was accountable to black people and their fight for justice."[20]

Cone delivered his first public essay on Black Theology at Elmhurst College in 1968. He spoke on "Christianity and Black Power." He was not interested in a white, distorted version of faith that neglected the struggle of black liberation. Cone reflects:

If Christ was not to be found in black people's struggle for freedom, if he were not found in the ghettos with rat-bitten black children, if he were in rich white churches and their seminaries, then I wanted no part of him.[21]

Cone's essay was a radical manifesto that identified the struggle for Black Power with the Gospel. Black Power, he argued, is not at odds with the Gospel; it *is* the Gospel for the American Church. For Cone, Black Power is nothing less than the expression of black people who are tired of being "exploited and humiliated."[22] Black theology developed out of the cry of black blood, the struggle for liberty that began four-hundred years ago.

Malcolm X quickly became a strong influence in Cone's life. He writes, "Malcolm X revolutionized my consciousness, transforming me from a Negro theologian to a *black* theologian, angry and ready to do battle with white theology."[23] Cone's early work developed out of the need for a "theological revolution that could stand alongside Black Power."[24] Cone's essay was a public declaration of independence from the chains of white theology. He would no longer do theology for the approval of the white theological elites.

When white people heard Cone's identification of the Gospel with Black Power, they heard hatred towards white people rather than love for blackness and black dignity. But Cone always stressed that Black Power means "black people asserting the humanity that white supremacy denied."[25] Thus, it is a Christian responsibility to affirm Black Power against the oppression of white supremacy.

Cone was aware of the ideological perils lurking behind such an identification. As a student of Barth, he knew full well the danger of confusing a historical-political movement with divine revelation. Yet he wanted to disrupt the status quo and throw down the gauntlet against white supremacy. He saw himself standing closer to Barth than those American theologians who had domesticated Barth for their cause. They had used Barth as an excuse to do nothing in the face of racial injustice and to feel better about their privileged indifference to the struggle of liberation.

In 1969, Cone published *Black Theology and Black Power,* a powerful critique of white theology that pulled no punches in calling the white church anti-Christ, sinful, and heretical. Cone said it was "a therapeutic and a liberating experience" to write.[26] And he later said that it "saved my life as a theologian, allowing me to fulfill the true purpose of my calling."[27] The book expounded upon the arguments of his essay, mainly the claim that "Jesus and Black Power were advocating the same thing."[28] The righteous anger and undiluted social realism of Cone's work was a challenge white people could not ignore, and it remains vital today.

Cone moved from Adrian to teach at Union Theological Seminary in New York. He chose Union because it was near the largest black community in America, Harlem, but also because Union was home to the leading figureheads of white theology (Niebuhr in particular but also Tillich formerly). He remained at Union for the rest of his life.

White theologians, with only a few exceptions, were not pleased with Cone's book, but this should be no surprise. Cone remains a controversial figure to this day. "The oppressed claiming the right to do their own theology is always rejected by oppressors."[29]

What was a surprise, however, was the response of black theologians. While most were enthusiastic about *Black Theology and Black Power*, one of the key concerns was whether or not Cone was actually doing black theology, but white theology painted black. They criticized Cone for leaning too heavily on European theologians. Cone admitted there was something in this critique, saying it was a "bitter pill to swallow."[30] Cone's next few books, especially *The Spirituals and the Blues,* were his response to this critique. He showed a conscious effort to move away from any Euro-centric basis. And while Cone acknowledges the influence of Barth, Tillich, and Bonhoeffer on his work, he stressed, "At no point did a European theologian, not even Barth, control what I said about the gospel and the black struggle for freedom."[31] The primary source for black theology is the black experience and their enduring struggle for liberation. Cone explains, "I wanted to be a faithful witness to the redemptive meaning of nearly 400 years of black people suffering."[32]

While Cone has his reasons for distancing himself from dialectical theology, I read him as an heir of Karl Barth *par excellence.* That does not mean I see Cone as a Barthian, living in Barth's shadow—far from it! Instead, a true Barthian goes *beyond* Barth, and Cone's use of Barth qualifies as one of the most exceptional. Cone once compared his use of Barth to B. B. King's use of his favored guitar, Lucille, "I wasn't following Barth; he was simply an instrument I played and left behind whenever it got in my way."[33] Undoubtedly, Cone's relationship with European theology is complex, but few theologians have offered such a relentless challenge to the status quo. Just as Barth gives us a new way of doing theology, so Cone provides a new way of relating theology to its social and political environment. Bonhoeffer and Tillich also bear a strong influence on Cone, but I use the comparison with Barth to make a clear point.

Cone is closer to the real Barth than the domesticated Barth of white evangelicals, who import their anti-revolutionary ideologies into his theology. As a student of Barth, Cone is among his best, most creative, and most important. In American universities, especially, it is a tragedy that Cone is often just a footnote. He is sometimes even treated as if he were a voice of lesser importance than the liberation theologies that developed in Latin America. Yet this is undoubtedly the product of white academia's privileged blindness.

The same is true for Bonhoeffer. It is baffling to watch white Evangelicals idolize Bonhoeffer yet demonize Cone, a theologian who should be considered more important to America because he wrestled with a present evil (racism) and not a distant one (Nazism). It is likely because Cone confronted the sin within our hearts and Bonhoeffer an abstract evil on another continent that Americans reject the former and celebrate the latter. But I will step off my soapbox for now. There will be plenty of time to show precisely why I think Cone deserves more attention than he receives from American theology.

After the success of his first book, Cone began to realize, "God must have been preparing me for this vocation, that is, the task of leveling the most devastating black critique possible against the white church and its theology."[34] With every book, essay, and lecture that followed, Cone systematically dismantled white Christianity's unholy alliance with white supremacy. In its place, he developed a black theology of liberation. Cone argues, "Any theology in America that fails to engage white supremacy and God's liberation of black people from that evil is not Christian theology but a theology of the Antichrist."[35]

Cone wrote *Black Theology and Black Power* as "an attack on racism in white churches and an attack on self-loathing in black churches."[36] His next book, *A Black Theology of Liberation*, addressed white theology more directly. Yet it was rooted in the "Black Spirit" crying out for freedom. Cone would write every night after a long day of teaching, often with the blues and spirituals playing softly. He recalls, "The first sentence I wrote startled me: 'Christian theology is a theology of liberation.' No one had ever said that before. It became the core of my theology."[37] Cone cites the exodus event, the prophets, and Jesus as the three voices that defined for him the meaning of liberation.[38] To say that Christian theology is a theology of liberation is not hyperbole, but a Biblical and theological truth that has been ignored by white theology in favor of more abstract, philosophical concepts. But it is clear from the Scriptures that God has always been, and always will be, the God of history. God is involved in the struggle of the oppressed for liberation. That explains why Cone often claimed that the central message of the Bible is "God's liberation of poor from oppression."[39] Overwhelmingly, Cone was coming to see that "a Christian theologian couldn't be on the side of the oppressor."[40]

Black theology is not primarily an abstract academic discipline, but a theology of and for the black Church. Cone writes, "Its chief task is to help the church to be faithful to the task of preaching and living the liberating gospel of Jesus Christ in the world today."[41] It is a theology that refuses to remain trapped in pure knowledge without leading to love for the least of these. The question that matters most is not what we know but how we use what we know to liberate the oppressed. Cone writes, "Love demands that we participate in their liberation struggle, fighting against the forces of oppression."[42] Theology must lead to praxis.

Black theology thus emerged out of the black Church and its struggle for liberation. As Cone concludes, "It is and must remain a theology of and for black people arising out of the active political struggle to create a just society in order to bear witness to the coming of God's kingdom."[43] When black revolutionaries called theologians and preachers to take up arms against white racists, Cone responded that he "could not participate in a revolution that did not include my mother!"[44] He remembers one particularly disturbing statement from David Hilliard at the NCBC Convocation in Oakland. Hilliard warned that "unless [black preachers] were prepared to put down the Bible and pick up the gun to shoot white policemen, then he and other Panthers would shoot them as they shoot policemen."[45] From this, Cone realized the "extent to which white oppression had twisted the minds of our revolutionary leaders."[46] Instead, Cone believed that black liberation must remain committed to the black Church. That is why he never joined ranks with the black nationalist, black panthers, or any other revolutionary group.

The question that haunted Cone's youth, the problem of black suffering and God's justice, returned with a vengeance in 1973 with the publication of William Jones' *Is God a White Racist?* The book challenged black theology to consider the problem of theodicy more seriously. Cone summarizes the challenge: "If God is liberating black people from oppression, where is the empirical evidence to warrant that claim?"[47] Cone realized there is no answer to the problem of theodicy that would satisfy anyone outside of the black community of faith; even for the faithful, the question remains unresolved. Instead, Cone writes:

> Faith in Christ therefore does not explain evil; it empowers us to fight against evil. Faith prevents compromise and despair in the encounter with evil. But faith does not make evil acceptable or account for its existence. Evil remains inexplicable, not in spite of faith but because of it. In the struggle against evil, we encounter the 'crucified God' (Jürgen Moltmann's phrase) in the suffering of the victims of history.[48]

Evil is not a problem to be understood logically; it is a wound to be healed by love and justice. But if evil is an "open wound" in human history, it is *God's* wound. Cone writes, "The pain of the oppressed is God's pain, for he takes their suffering as his own, thereby freeing them from its ultimate control of their lives."[49] Thus, God's voice cries out in the cries of the poor and weak who suffer injustice. God suffers with them in their pain; every act of oppression is a sin against God. God's co-suffering love is a source of strength for the oppressed to resist their oppression, and Christ's resurrection means their efforts will not be in vain.

These reflections signify a shift beginning to occur in Cone's thought, culminating in the publication of his most systematic and mature work, *God of the Oppressed*. His work began to take on a universal tone while never leaving its central concern for black liberation. Cone argued that God identifies Godself unreservedly with the plight of the suffering, weak, poor, and oppressed. In dialogue with third world theologies, Cone realized it would not be enough to struggle for black liberation in America if that means ignoring the struggles of the oppressed throughout the world. Evil is evil, no matter where it is found. Thus, liberation became a universal goal, not merely an American one. Cone writes:

> The universal dimension of the gospel was revealed in the particularities of poor people throughout the world. [...] While there is no knowledge of Jesus' gospel apart from the particular struggles of the poor for liberation, we must never absolutize a particular struggle (whether black, African, Asian, or Latin) to the exclusion of others.[50]

Racism, sexism, imperialism, and capitalism are interconnected systems; fighting injustice means overcoming all forms of oppression.

Through his dialogue with third-world theologies, Cone became more familiar with Marx's analysis of class and capital. He realized that racism and capitalism are twin demons. His theology also began to converse with other liberationists, including feminists, and take them seriously. Cone summarizes well the central conviction of his mature writing: "I contend that any theological perspective that does not remain committed to the liberation of victims cannot be Christian."[51] It is a vision he remained faithful to for the rest of his life.

One day, while Cone was teaching at Union, a student stood up and shouted from the back of the room, "Dr. Cone, you don't know a God damn thing about the gay experience!"[52] It was like a flashback to Cone's outburst twenty years earlier. But unlike his racist professor, Cone was not angry. He knew the young man was right and realized that homophobia affected him in a similar way that he had suffered from white supremacy. Cone wisely replied:

> Your anger is how theology begins. It starts with anger about a great contradiction that can't be ignored. That's what happened to Athanasius in the fourth century, Luther in the sixteenth, and Barth in the twentieth. It also happened to me. If I had not been angry about white supremacy, I would not have written anything.[53]

Cone once described himself as the "angriest theologian in America,"[54] and a cursory glance through his books reveals why. His work remains sharply focused and critical, like a knife systematically cutting away at a cancerous tumor. Cone spent his entire life courageously devoted to preaching the Gospel of God's liberation of the poor from oppression. This dedication began with a clear focus on the liberation of poor blacks from white supremacy, but as he matured, Cone's work expanded to include *all* victims of oppression. So he extolled the young, outbursting student in his classroom, "Embrace your experience! Then write your heart out."[55] The cause of liberation is all-encompassing. Cone's pioneering work in developing black theology paves the way for future theologies of liberation to overthrow the systemic oppression of the poor and weak, wherever they may be found. Whether it is the struggle for LGBTQ+ liberation, the cries of abused women in the #metoo movement, or the class struggle of the poor against capitalism, Cone reminds us that their struggle is also God's struggle.

God is the God of the oppressed and takes sides with the weak and poor in the liberation struggle. There is no one-side-fits-all theology. Theology begins with experience, as Cone writes, "No theologian—past or present—can replace the need to do theology for one's self."[56] This is not to imply that the struggle for black liberation must give way to a new battle. Indeed, "Black blood is crying out to God all over this land."[57] The struggle for black liberation goes on still today. But it has also paved the way for countless other victims of oppression to take liberation into their own hands.

James Cone died on April 28, 2018. He lived to be 79. His voice is a lasting prophetic beacon for the next generation of theologians who dare to fight for liberation. That voice echoes still in the world-wide theological movement he helped create and foster, liberation theology generally and black theology particularly. His legacy is perhaps more vital now than it has ever been, and it lives on in profound ways through the work of his students, friends, and even his enemies who can no longer afford to ignore him.

1

BLACK THEOLOGY AND WHITE THEOLOGY

Summary: White theology thinks it can speak for all people and times, and it is thus a heretical, racist illusion. All theology is contextual. Theology is never color-blind or apolitical because it is bound to actual human conditions. It is political language, written either from the perspective of the oppressor or the oppressed. Any theology unconcerned with the least of these is not *Christian* theology.

In Cone's words:

> White theology is not Christian theology because the language about God in white theology is derived from the culture of white supremacy. To understand Christianity from the dominant point of view is like trying to understand Jesus from the Roman point of view.[1]

> Christian theology is a theology of liberation. It is a rational study of the being of God in the world in light of the existential situation of an oppressed community, relating the forces of liberation to the essence of the gospel, which is Jesus Christ. This means that its sole reason for existence is to put into ordered speech the meaning of God's activity in the world, so that the community of the oppressed will recognize that its inner thrust for liberation is not only *consistent with* the gospel but *is* the

gospel of Jesus Christ. There can be no Christian theology that is not identified unreservedly with those who are humiliated and abused.[2]

Secondary quotes:

Thus absolute revelation, for Cone, is universal, but because there is no universalism without being particular, any treatment of absolute revelation must root itself in a particular, concrete human condition, that is, the condition of the oppressed.[3]

— HARRY H. SINGLETON, III

The success of liberation theology lay in challenging the long-held explicit methods and goals of theology, redefining the relationship between religion and politics in a new theo-political space, and altering the expectations for the role of religion in social change rather than legitimation.[4]

— LILIAN CALLES BARGER

Introduction

One of the distinguishing features of liberation theology is its focus on the context from which theology is written. All theology is contextual language bound to a particular time, place, and people. The illusion of white theology is its supposed political neutrality and theological objectivity. White theology is thus culpable for the racist system it supports with its silence. Refusing to confront the sin of racism is the same as affirming it. Neutrality is a white illusion; it is sinful to do nothing in the face of racism. We are guilty of supporting a system of injustice whenever we fail to adopt a staunchly antiracist position. Neutrality only helps the oppressor.

In this chapter, we will examine the differences between white and black theology. The nature of theology and its relation to politics is a vital aspect of what makes black theology unique. Cone's work is frequently rejected by critics who argue that he wrongly injects a political ideology into theology. In contrast, I hope to show that Cone's theology is so polit-ical *because* it is so profoundly theological. His work is revolutionary because it is rooted in the politics of Jesus Christ, not because it has some hidden commitment to a political ideology (such as Marxism). It is not Cone who fails to be theological but white theology in its political neutrality that fails to take Christ's Gospel seriously.

Contextual theology

White theology is theology written from the perspective of whiteness. No one consciously sets out to write "white theology." But any theology that lends support to the status quo and is more concerned with minor doctrinal points than the suffering of the poor and oppressed is a kind of white theology. In that sense, we may also call white theology "privileged theology" because it develops from the dominant perspective. It is ultimately a difference in allegiance. White theology is the theology of oppressors, who either silently or actively lend their support to systems of oppression. Because white people benefit from black oppression, it is easier for us to be silent in the face of white supremacy. But the Gospel calls us to fight against injustice, even—and especially—the injustices we benefit from.

White theology does not have to think about race. That is why it seldom considers racism a theological issue worthy of sustained consideration. Every year, millions of sermons, conferences, and books are produced by the white, American Church. But how many confront the sin of racism? Because it does not concern them directly, because it challenges their comfortable way of life, racism does not often merit white theological attention. And that is the sin of white theology: silence in the face of ongoing injustice. But in a world plagued by racism, white theology's color-blindness is nothing less than implicit allegiance to white supremacy. Indeed, white supremacy, not Christ's Gospel, is the controlling ideology of white theology.

Two racist assumptions are behind why theology's failure to take racism seriously. First, white theology assumes that we must ignore personal history, cultural bias, and racial identity to be "objective" and "scientific." But this is impossible. We cannot step outside of ourselves and do theology as if we were an indifferent, passive observer to history and culture. We cannot circumvent our biases. Theology is a human pursuit, and pretending to ignore this fact in the name of "objective" truth is nothing less than intellectual dishonesty. Theology is about God, but God does not write theology; humans do. Thus, theology is bound to the contextual limitations of the people who write it.

The second racist assumption is the foundation of the first. White theology acts as if it can ignore race because whiteness is presumed to be the "default" perspective. Thus, white theologians claim that race has nothing to do with theology because *their race* is culturally and politically perceived as the default way of being human, which they wrongly assume privies them to a universal, objective point of view. In reality, white theology is nothing less than a theology of oppressors.

Few white theologian take their whiteness as anything other than the default starting position; they assume they can access objective truth without critically examining their implicit biases. But this is a racist assumption, which causes white theologians to imagine that they have not *already* included their whiteness in theological pursuits.

Black theology challenges the supposed universalism of white theology by establishing the black experience as a valid source for theological thought, asserting the contextual limitations of theology. The interplay between the universal and particular is key. While Cone asserts the traditional idea that revelation is universal, that God remains constant, he nonetheless counterbalances this notion with the equally essential factor of human contextual limitations. The universal is inaccessible apart from the particular. Thus, theology must be contextual.

White theologians fail to see that their whiteness is a biased perspective that hinders their ability to understand the Gospel and affects the way they do theology. Thus, they think they do not need to think about race. But race is *always already* an issue in theology because the men and women who do theology cannot overcome their limited perspective any more than they might leap over their own shadow. Race matters because we live in a world that still divides people by their skin tone.[5] But historically, there is only one privileged racial perspective that has had a voice. To ignore humanity's beautiful diversity and consider whiteness to be the "objective" or "universal" point of view is the sin of white theology. It is a sure sign of white privilege whenever a theologian claims they can speak for God without first being clear about the bias of whiteness. By leaving these biases unexamined, then turning to criticize black theology's clarity regarding how race affects theology, white theologians have been complicit in racist aggressions against non-whites, attempting to erase their history and culture.

In the 1986 preface to *A Black Theology of Liberation,* Cone drives this point home:

> Theology is not universal language about God. Rather, it is human speech informed by historical and theological traditions, and written for particular times and places. Theology is *contextual* language—that is, defined by the human situation that gives birth to it. No one can write theology for all times, places, and persons.[6]

The history of theology has been primarily the history of *white theology*. The emergence of black theology, with other theologies of liberation, challenges the death-grip of white supremacy. Almost exclusively, the white, male, middle-class perspective has dominated the conversation. But as Cone argues, a privileged perspective is more likely to distort the Gospel than understand it rightly. In contrast, black theology is theology arising from the underclass.

Theology written in the comfort of a safe, suburban neighborhood is radically different from theology written in the horrors of the slums and ghettos. The circumstances of life drastically affect how we think about God. As Moltmann realized, "Reading the Bible with the eyes of the poor is a different thing from reading it with the eyes of the man with a full belly."[7] The community of the poor and oppressed are better suited to know the God of the oppressed. That is why Cone argues that the black perspective more faithfully expresses God's liberating activity. White theology distorts the Gospel, and black theology is an attempt to return to a more *Christian* contextual framework—namely, the perspective of the least of these—so that we might better understand the Gospel.

Under the supremacy of whiteness, theology has been a playground for those in power to tell those without power what to think about God. But we must ask ourselves: Who is better positioned to understand the Gospel, the oppressor or the oppressed? Is Christ found today with the privileged and wealthy, or the poor, weak, and powerless? White theology has claimed to be the sole guardian of God's truth. Yet the privileged see the world in a perverted way. They think society is mostly good and acceptable; everything is fine from where they stand. But from the perspective of the underclass, life on Earth is hell. Of course, those in power—who are only in power because they exploit those without power—deem the status quo acceptable. But it is hell for those without power *because* it is heaven for their oppressors.

Black theology and white theology differ because they arise from different social, political, and economic situations. Our personal experiences unavoidably establish a mental framework for how we interpret the Gospel. Thus, white theology has favored political neutrality because white supremacy benefits whites. White people have inherited a world that privileges them unduly, but, whether they are aware of this or not, it favors them at the expense of oppressing others. It is in their best interest to remain silent about the sins of white supremacy. Neutrality always helps the oppressor and does nothing for the oppressed. White theology is written from the perspective of the privileged, and thus it has fundamentally misunderstood the Gospel of Jesus Christ.

Black theology does not have the luxury of political indifference. For black people in America and around the world, suffering, oppression, marginalization, and poverty are inescapable, daily realities. The cries of black blood go unheeded by white theologians, but black theology cannot ignore the suffering of their ancestors. Whites do not own the Christian faith, nor do the rich or the male. Black theology challenges white theology's supremacy by arguing that it has failed theologically to know Christ because it has failed to know the least of these. It has failed to listen to their cries of anguish, which is also the voice of Christ crying out in their midst for justice. White theology has turned its back on Christ in neglecting the least of these. Thus, the heresy of white theology must die for the sake of black theology; the theology of the oppressors must make way for the theology of the oppressed.

The political God

God is not nor has ever been politically neutral in the face of evil. The God of the Bible is a political God. However, political neutrality is the comfortable illusion of white Christianity, and it has caused us to become blind to God's concern for the least of these.

What is a Christian's political obligation? How should a believer engage in politics? It is not to look out for one's self-interests. Instead, a Christian is one whose political duty belongs to the poor, the weak, and the oppressed. Yet this has not historically been the case. Christians frequently situate themselves with Herod and Caesar and thus stand in the way of God's revolution in the stables and on the cross.

We must forgo the illusion of neutrality and come to terms with the political obligations made explicit in Christ's teachings, ethics, and lifestyle. Theology that is concerned with Jesus of Nazareth is necessarily concerned with the politics of the underprivileged and oppressed.

For white people, especially in America, it is often taboo to speak of politics. When another mass shooting occurs in an American school, a common refrain is, "Now is not the time to make this tragedy about politics." But if we ignore the systemic issues that *caused* the problem, will it ever be resolved? That would be like saying to a cancer patient: "I see your suffering and pain, but now is not the time to make this about cancer." The underlying cause of the problem remains unaddressed whenever we feign political neutrality. Neutrality is just as unreasonable as rampant injustice.

It is unfashionable, in a liberal society, to consider something a political issue. But this mindset only supports injustice. Most of the problems we face are *already* political. The prevalence of school shootings in America is the result of political policies. The tragedy itself may be hard to talk about, but if we continuously turn a blind eye to the issues facing our world, nothing will ever change. Symptoms reveal the disease, and it is only the fool who ignores the disease behind the symptom. That is why the rejection of all things political, the common claim that "I'm not political," and the idea that the Church is an apolitical institution are subtly racist ideas because, by our silence, we support the violence of the status quo. *Silence is violence.* Black men and women are regularly lynched by police in the streets of America, or thrown in jail at an alarmingly high rate, or robbed of their potential and their children's potential because of white supremacy and the policies it upholds. Despite American's odd rejection of all things political, politics are essential to human life. To be silent in the face of injustice is to be guilty of injustice. The moment people organize, there are political implications to their activities. The Church, too, is an unavoidably political institution for this reason.

Theologians always write theology in and for a particular community. White theology has historically served only the interests of the powerful, rich, and privileged. But that is not the community to which Christ came. The incarnation reveals God's preferential option for the poor. God was not born in Herod's courts but into poverty, oppression, and exclusion.

White theology's great sin is its silence. Where were white theologians during slavery? While some notable figures spoke out against it, the majority either explicitly or implicitly supported the violence done to African slaves. And where is white theology today?

One-third of black children in America are born into poverty, compared to one in ten white children.[8] One-third of all black men will end up behind bars sometime in their lives.[9] Police routinely and systematically target poor, black neighborhoods,[10] and are prone to more severe acts of violence against black bodies than white bodies, killing black bodies three times more often.[11] The war on drugs is a colossal failure, which initially targeted black people, as one of Nixon's top advisors admitted.[12] Black families are far more likely to live in neighborhoods with inadequate air and water quality.[13]

There is no denying on a factual and statistical level the prevalence of racism in American society. Where is white theology in these injustices? The sad answer is that it has been responsible for maintaining the status quo because whiteness benefits from the system as it is. To confront that system requires renouncing our privileged position in society. The white Church is too ideologically committed to white supremacy to accept its sinfulness at face value.

White theology has interpreted the message of Jesus according to its privileged concerns. Cone pointedly writes, "Because white theologians live in a society that is racist, the oppression of black people does not occupy an important item on their theological agenda."[14] White theology unfairly prioritizes selfish concerns over the cries of the poor and helpless, turning a deaf ear and a blind eye to the sufferings of this world on a practical level. Theologians are happy to discuss theodicy on a theoretical level. But when confronted with actual suffering, especially when they are implicitly its cause, it is too political to concern them.

It is common to criticize James Cone for mixing theology and politics, but the truth is the two disciplines are inseparably intertwined. We cannot do theology in a vacuum, as if it is a purely theoretical pursuit. Is not the God we serve a God of justice? Was Jesus Christ not the champion of the poor and oppressed? It is baffling how quickly white theologians reject Cone for injecting politics into theology when the Bible is overwhelmingly concerned with politics. In a racist society, neutrality is a sin because it supports racism by letting it go on unchallenged. As Christ reminds us: "Truly I tell you, just as you did it to one of the least of these who are members of my family, you did it to me. [...] Truly I tell you, just as you did not do it to one of the least of these, you did not do it to me" (Matthew 25:40, 45).

White theology has committed theological heresy by ignoring the political imperatives of the Gospel. White theologians discuss Cone's work as if theology and politics have no bearing on one another. But this, in itself, is to deny the incarnation in a docetic manner. God became a man and entered into our midst *because* God is deeply concerned about human affairs, which necessarily includes the policies that structure society. Theology and politics are inseparable in the same way that theology without ethics is bankrupt. God is concerned with the human condition. It is not Cone who fails to be theological by taking humanity's political situation seriously; white theologians fail when they bury their heads in the sand and pretend they can ignore God's deep concern for the least of these. The God of the Bible is the political God. Theology is necessarily political.

Revelation means liberation

God reveals Godself in the event of liberation. For the Israelites, God defined Godself according to liberation from Egyptian captivity. And according to Cone, God is still revealed in the historical liberation of oppressed people everywhere. His doctrine of revelation asserts an integral link between revelation and liberation. That means God is not an object we observe passively. God is not a philosophical idea or an unmoved principle. Instead, God is active in the plight of the oppressed, fighting for their liberation.

We have seen how liberation theology is contextually bound to a particular community and their liberation struggle. Cone argues further that theology is not rightly *Christian* theology unless it is rooted firmly in the perspective of the poor and oppressed, the community Christ called His own. We cannot know God if we ignore the least of these. God is revealed in the event of liberation.

Thus, if we want to know God, we must understand the struggles of oppressed people. By joining the plight of the poor, we encounter the God who raised Christ from the dead, having first raised Israel from slavery in Egypt. Singleton explains, "To know God is to know of God's activity of liberation on behalf of the oppressed. God's revelation means liberation, an emancipation from the political, economic, and social structures of society."[15]

All theology is bound to a particular context. White theology is just as limited to its perspective as black theology. But we must realize that God is not equally accessible to all perspectives. There is a specific context in which God has decided to reveal Godself to humanity. According to Cone, the proper context from which we can know God is the community of the oppressed. Of course, God is universally knowable, but in the incarnation, God bound Godself to a particular context. We cannot circumvent the particular in the name of an abstract universal. God is not a philosophical problem to be solved but the God who became a specific man, Jesus of Nazareth, and identified with an oppressed community, the Israelites under Roman occupation. Cone explains:

> God is found in the midst of blacks fighting for dignity, justice, and respect. God is present in people struggling for life, and not in the abstract metaphysical world of reason, which is only inhabited by philosophers and theologians and other privileged intellectuals. The Christian God is not the God of the philosophers, not the God of Plato, Kant, and Hegel, but rather, the God of the Exodus, and the Prophets, and of Jesus. If God is in the world where people are abused and exploited, what then is God doing? That was my question, as I wrestle with the fire burning inside me and in the ghettos of America's cities. Christians are called by God to plunge themselves into the world on behalf of those who are voiceless and hurt.[16]

Cone's doctrine of revelation implies that white theology, the theology of the oppressor, is unable to recognize God as the liberator of the oppressed because they benefit from the systems of oppression. Their context blinds them from seeing God's liberating activity among the poor and weak. The God of white theology is not the same God revealed in and by Jesus Christ. Thus, white theology is heretical not only in its ethical affiliation with white supremacy but in so far as it professes a different God. Their God is not the God of liberation but rather the upholder of the status quo, a God who condones injustice and sides with the privileged and powerful. In short, the God of white theology is an idol.

Whenever theology fails to speak for the poor and oppressed, it is no longer Christian theology. As Cone writes:

> Whatever else Christian theology must be, it must take sides with the victims who are economically and politically oppressed. If theology does not side with the victims of economic injustice, it cannot represent *the Victim,* Jesus of Nazareth, who was crucified because he was a threat to the political and religious structures of his time.[17]

Christianity became the official state religion of Rome under

Constantine. The Church transitioned from a position of weakness as the oppressed minority to dominance as the wielders of state power. Accordingly, Christian thinking lost the critical notion of God's preferential self-revealing to the oppressed. The Church's fidelity to the poor faltered.

Today, the meaning of Christianity is commonly defined according to the priorities of the first-world. Thus, it is easy to lose sight of the revolutionary aspect of Christ's solidarity with the poor and weak. Yet God did not incarnate into the courts of Herod but the stables of Bethlehem. God did not identify with the rich rulers but with the man from Nazareth who had no place to lay his head.

If we are privileged and powerful in society, it can be easy to overlook Christ's radical solidarity with the powerless and the underprivileged. We will never find what we are not looking for, and the privileged seldom pursue an understanding of their sinful complicity in injustice. Trying to understand the Gospel in America from the white-perspective is like trying to understand Jesus from the perspective of the Roman soldiers. It is not impossible—with God all things are possible (see Matthew 19:16-30)—but until white, rich, dominant people repent of their privileges, it is unlikely they will see the Gospel of God's liberating activity among the poor, oppressed, and black. It was difficult for the rich young ruler to enter the Kingdom of God, so today, it is hard for the powerful, privileged, and wealthy to know the Gospel of Jesus.

Cone's doctrine of revelation argues that God is known only in the communities of the oppressed. In his American context, this means that God's revelation is found among the black community. Cone explains:

> Revelation is God's self-disclosure to humankind *in the context of liberation.* To know God is to know God's work of liberation on behalf of the oppressed. God's revelation means liberation, an emancipation from death-dealing political, economic, and social structures of society. This is the essence of biblical revelation.[18]

Theology is not genuinely *Christian* theology unless it arises from the context of an oppressed community, the same community Christ called His own. For Cone, revelation is the act of God to liberate the victims of oppression. Thus, the black experience is a form of God's self-revelation to America.

As I write this chapter, the streets of every major American city (including Columbus, Ohio, my home) are overflowing with angry men and women, rioting in protest against police brutality because of the lynching of George Floyd. A white police officer killed Floyd on May 25, 2020. The white officer set his knee on Floyd's neck for eight minutes as Floyd cried out for help, suffered, and died. White theology cannot know the God of the oppressed because its knee remains on the neck of the black and powerless despite their cries for help. These are God's cries. God died with George Floyd. God suffered and suffocated at the hands of white supremacy. Floyd's last cries for help are the cries of the oppressed, reverberating now in the rioting and looting and burning of America's cities.

The radical conclusion we must draw from Cone's theology is that these cries of unrest are God's Word to white America. It is a call for us to repent of white supremacy and turn to the God of the poor and powerless. The Gospel is being proclaimed anew through the anger of these protesters. White supremacy, the white theology that supports it, and the silent white Churches that do nothing in the face of injustice are culpable; they murdered God in the death of George Floyd.

Sources of revelation

Cone argues that black theology, arising from an oppressed community, is better situated to understand the original context of the Gospel. In contrast, white theology arises from a privileged perspective like that of the Romans who killed Jesus and is thus unable to comprehend Christ's Gospel of liberation. It is a matter of social, political, and economic status and how it impacts theological thought. Cone explains:

> The dissimilarity between Black Theology and white theology lies at the point of each having different mental grids which account for their different approaches to the gospel. [...] This means that theology is political language. What people think about God, Jesus Christ, and the Church cannot be separated from their own social and political status in a given society.[19]

God reveals Godself in the liberating experiences of the oppressed. That is why the black experience is an essential source of revelation in Cone's theology. If God reveals Godself in the context of the oppressed, then oppressed communities are a form of God's revelation on the Earth. For Cone, the black experience is not necessarily a *foundational* source for theology, as Jesus Christ is, but it is nonetheless an essential source we cannot overlook. In many ways, Cone echoes Barth's concept of the three-fold Word of God here, though he takes the idea into new territory. Cone never consciously makes this comparison, but I think it will be helpful.

Barth posited three forms of the Word of God. These are separated into *primary* revelation and *secondary witnesses* to revelation. Jesus Christ alone is direct revelation, the infallible Word of God incarnate. The fallible, secondary (or mediated) forms of the Word of God are Holy Scripture and preaching. We have access to direct revelation only through the mediated witness of Scripture and preaching, but these forms truly become God's Word as God speaks in and through them. Thus, secondary forms of the Word of God are not in themselves God's Word but *become* God's Word by the Spirit.[20]

It will be instructive to examine Cone's understanding of these secondary witnesses to revelation because of the issues involved in his elevation of the black experience as a source of divine revelation.

The Bible

The Bible is not an infallible witness. On this point, both Cone and Barth agree. Cone explains: "God was not the author of the Bible, nor were its writers mere secretaries. Efforts to prove verbal inspiration of the scriptures result from the failure to see the real meaning of the biblical message: human liberation!"[21] For Cone, the concept of biblical inerrancy is an exercise in missing the point. While the white Church spends its time wondering if Jonah actually entered the belly of a whale, "the state is enacting inhuman laws against the oppressed."[22] Thus, for Cone, the point of reading the Bible is not to be convinced of its accuracy, but to be confronted with its radical message of liberation. "It matters little to the oppressed who authored scripture; what is important is whether it can serve as a weapon against oppressors."[23]

White supremacy is less offensive to white theologians than the rejection of inerrancy. That is obvious from the way white theology discusses these two issues. Inerrancy is passionately enforced, but white supremacy is seldom taken seriously. But these issues are not the same: confessing an imperfect Bible did not lead to enslaving, brutalizing, and murdering millions based on their skin; white supremacy did. And while white supremacy continues to commit similar atrocities, white theology silently supports it. Slaveholders used the inerrancy of Scripture to support slavery, and the idea is still used today to deny liberation to the oppressed. White theology is anti-Christian in its priorities and practices.

The Bible, for both Cone and Barth, is a witness to the Word of God, not the Word in itself. Thus, the point is not the accuracy of a book—although both theologians affirm its reliability and trustworthiness—but rather, the point is hearing the Word of God through the human, fallible witness of the Bible. The point is hearing the Word and also *doing* the Word. White theology has so fetishized the accuracy of a book that it has, like the Pharisees, overlooked the weightier matters of the law, such as justice, mercy, and faith (Matthew 23:23). In Christ's words, "Woe to you, scribes and Pharisees, hypocrites!" Indeed, woe to the white Church and its theologians, who fret over the accuracy of a book but neglect the desperate cries for justice from the lips of the poor and oppressed!

Preaching and the black experience

The third form of the Word of God, for Barth, is preaching. Like the Bible, preaching is a witness to God's Word that becomes the Word of God by grace. It is here that Cone swaps preaching for the black experience. And rightfully so, since both preaching and the black experience involve a community attempting to bear witness to God's self-revelation. These are also subject to the relative authority of Scripture, which is subject to the absolute authority of Jesus Christ.

This comparison explains why Cone considered the black experience a source of revelation for black theology. It is functionally no different than what Barth has already done by considering preaching a form of the Word of God,[24] and critics of Cone have seldom recognized the potential of this insight. The witness of the community is vital for any doctrine of the Word since the event of divine revelation does not take place in a vacuum. Theology is always written in a particular context and for particular people. To ignore this fact is to fall back into the trap of white theology and its false objectivity. And as Cone argues, because God has chosen to identify in Christ with the least of these, the poor and oppressed, then it is only in the community of the oppressed that we may encounter divine revelation, the Word of God.

Cone makes an important distinction:

[L]ike Scripture, the black experience is a *source* of the Truth but not the

Truth itself. Jesus Christ is the Truth and thus stands in judgment over all statements about truth.[25]

The black experience points beyond itself to the Truth without being the truth itself. As T. F. Torrance explains, the error of fundamentalism is the "identification of biblical statements about the truth with the truth itself to which they refer."[26] Note the distinction between statements *about* truth and the Truth itself. The black experience is a form of the Word of God because its statements point to the Truth without being identified with it. Thus, it is a valid *source* of divine revelation, yet Cone does not confuse it with revelation itself. He is not idealizing the black experience beyond any point of criticism. Cone was frequently critical of the black Church, but he was also committed to hearing God's Word spoken in and through their struggles for liberation.

God does not identify with abstract principles but with God's acts towards us in Jesus Christ and history. It is worth briefly noting how Cone shares the actualist theme that dominates Barth's theology. Barth's actualism was identified and defined by George Hunsinger, who writes, "At the most general level [actualism] means that he thinks primarily in terms of events and relationship rather than monadic or self-contained substances."[27] This includes the denial of any "ahistorical" relationship with God. We cannot know God in a vacuum apart from the events of history precisely because God *identifies with* the event of God's disclosure in history. God corresponds to Godself. Thus, for Cone, the black community's lived experience in the struggle for historical liberation from oppression is a form of God's self-revelation. This actualist theme determines much of Barth's theology, but Cone takes it into new territory by making it even more concrete. Cone brilliantly unveils the value of Barth's insight by going beyond it.

The experience of black oppression in America is the revelation of God as God acts for their liberation. It is a Word of hope for the black people today suffering under oppression, and it is a Word of rebuke for the white people who must learn to see themselves as the oppressors of the poor, weak, and black. We must listen and hear the Word of God crying out in the cries of the powerless and poor.

Is black theology anti-white?

I want to conclude this chapter by addressing a common misconception about Cone's work. The harsh reality of Cone's critique comes off as a total rejection of all white-skinned people, but this is to ignore the unique way he uses the term "whiteness."

First, let us look at one of the best definitions of black theology, put forward by the National Committee of Black Churchmen on June 13, 1969:

> Black Theology is a theology of black liberation. It seeks to plumb the black condition in the light of God's revelation in Jesus Christ, so that the black community can see that the gospel is commensurate with the achievement of black humanity. Black Theology is a theology of 'blackness.' It is the affirmation of black humanity that emancipates black people from white racism, thus providing authentic freedom both for white and black people. It affirms the humanity of white people in that is says No to the encroachment of white oppression.
>
> The message of liberation is the revelation of God as revealed in the incarnation of Jesus Christ. Freedom IS the gospel. Jesus is the Liberator! [...] The demand that Christ the Liberator imposes on all men *requires* all blacks to affirm their full dignity as persons and all whites to surrender their presumptions of superiority and abuses of power.[28]

Black theology arises from the struggles of black people, but its particularity is also its universalism. Because God is for the liberation of black people from the bondage of white supremacy, God is also for the liberation of whites from the sin of whiteness. Black theology is *for* white people in the same way that the Gospel is for sinners. Thus, it *is* against "whiteness," but not white people. This distinction is vital.

Cone uses blackness and whiteness in both the physiological and, more importantly, in the ontological sense. Ontologically, blackness is a symbol of all oppressed people, and whiteness is a symbol of oppressors. Physiologically, black is the historical color of oppressed people, and white is the color of their oppressors. The ontological is universal, the physiological is particular, and they are dialectically connected. In other words, we could also say that "whiteness" is a mindset, and white skin is a physical trait that most often results in a mindset of whiteness. The two are not always the same, but white people often adopt whiteness by default. That is the contextual limitation we have been discussing in this chapter. Whiteness is the mindset of the oppressor, and people born with white skin often adapt themselves to that status. But the issue is whiteness, not white skin.

Burrow explains:

> What [Cone] rejected was whiteness, which is, among other things, the perverted attitude that persons with white skin are superior to blacks and other people of color. Cone did not reject persons with white skins, but persons whose attitude, mental outlook, and actions always lead to the exploitation of other persons and groups. Cone has never expressed hatred for white-skinned people in his writings or lectures, although he has always been aware that whiteness as a state of mind has generally been expressed by persons with white skins.[29]

Understanding Cone's symbolic use of whiteness helps us avoid hastily labeling his work "reverse racist." We will return to this point later on, but it is crucial to be precise. Often, white people accept their role in white supremacy uncritically and adopt the mindset of "whiteness" without real- izing they are part of a system that oppresses black people. Therefore, white people and whiteness are often synonymous. But it is not white skin in itself that is the issue, but the mindset of whiteness. The goal of black liberation is the release of black people from the bondage of white supremacy, and that includes the liberation of white people from their role as white oppressors.

Cone's work is not as clear as it could be regarding this distinction. He explained the difference as early as his second book, but it was hidden in a footnote. In *A Black Theology of Liberation,* Cone clarifies: "When I say that white theology is not Christian theology, I mean the theology that has been written without any reference to the oppressed of the land."[30] Interestingly, Cone says that his critique of white theology excludes theologians such as Barth and Bonhoeffer because they did theology from the perspective of the oppressed. Even Niebuhr, who was frequently criti- cized by Cone, "moves in the direction of blackness" with his book *Moral Man and Immoral Society.*[31] Cone is not rejecting white-skinned theolo- gians or deeming it a sin to be born white. It is a judgment against the mindset and ideological commitments of whites, not their skin tone.

Cone's lack of clarity about this distinction is not necessarily a flaw in his work. It is possible that he deliberately obscured the distinction from casual readers. John Bennett thinks Cone is intentionally ambiguous because he does not want to soften his critique of whiteness or to let whites off the hook.[32] White people are supposed to feel uncomfortable when reading Cone. Even if the main problem is whiteness and not white skin, the mindset of whiteness is most common among white-skinned people. Thus, it is perfectly valid, even necessary, for Cone to keep the distinction obscure because white people may try to excuse themselves from blame if they are not confronted directly. As a white person, I must reject the impulse to justify myself. I am not innocent and must be confronted with my sinful allegiance to whiteness. Cone's message is a wake-up call. But for clarity's sake, it is essential to recognize the distinction between white people and whiteness in Cone's work. The distinction excuses no one, but it clarifies why Cone's work is not anti-white in being against whiteness.

2

GOD IS BLACK

Summary: God is symbolically and ontologically black because the God revealed in Jesus Christ is the God of the oppressed. Cone takes the doctrine of God out of the realm of abstract speculation by focusing instead on God's being-in-act in the historical struggle for liberation. The doctrine of God cannot ignore its political and racial connotations. The neutral, apolitical, indifferent God of white theology is an unbiblical heresy. God's love is incomplete without justice; God is black.

In Cone's words:

The blackness of God, and everything implied by it in a racist society, is the heart of the black theology doctrine of God. There is no place in black theology for a colorless God in a society where human beings suffer precisely because of their color. [...] Either God is identified with the oppressed to the point that their experience becomes God's experience, or God is a God of racism. [...] The blackness of God means that God has made the oppressed condition God's own condition.[1]

God, according to the Bible, is known by what he does, and what he does is always related to the liberation of the oppressed.[2]

If theology does not side with the poor, then it cannot speak for Yahweh who is the God of the poor.[3]

Secondary quotes:

Just because God has no *literal* color does not mean that God may not have a *symbolic* color.[4]

— DENNIS W. WILEY

God is whoever raised Jesus from the dead, having before raised Israel from Egypt.[5]

— ROBERT W. JENSON

Introduction

James Cone's doctrine of God dismantles the racist assumptions that keep white supremacy in power. One such assumption is the claim that God is politically neutral, color-blind, and colorless. In other words, it is the unbiblical idea that God does not take sides. A God who does not take sides cannot be the liberator of the oppressed, the God of justice and love. God's historical identification with the plight of the Israelites disproves this idea.

The doctrine of God often says more about us than God. We tend to project our ideals up into heaven, magnifying them to the nth degree, and call them "God." But we also project our sin unto God, justifying our shortcomings by creating a feedback loop of divine approval. If our God is apolitical, then our apathy in the face of racism is justified. If our God is white and color-blind, then racism and white supremacy are acceptable Christian values. We suppose God is on the side of the powerful and wealthy. Thus, our violent disdain—including support for violent power structures such as the police and military—against weak and powerless people is divinely affirmed. The ideological possibilities are endless. We regularly justify ourselves by changing our God, rather than changing ourselves by encountering the God revealed in Christ.

The color of God matters. To place God on the side of the white, wealthy, male oppressor is theological malpractice. It is dangerous and sinful to align God with oppressive structures of power such as white supremacy, sexism, and capitalism. God is not the God of the powerful oppressors but of the poor and helpless. Thus, Cone reaches a startling but necessarily disruptive conclusion: God is black. Cone explains:

> In a society where blacks have been enslaved and segregated for nearly four centuries by whites because of their color and where evil has been portrayed as 'black' and good as 'white' in religious and cultural values, the idea that 'God is black' is not only theologically defensible, but is a necessary corrective against the powers of domination. A just and loving God cannot be identified with the values of evil people.[6]

In this chapter, we will explore the theological and biblical arguments for God's blackness. We will also further clarify the critical difference between physiological and ontological blackness, which is a vital distinction for understanding Cone's theology.

A colorless God?

White depictions of Jesus are so common that we no longer question them. Even though it is historically doubtful, many still assume Christ was white. Ask a random Christian to picture Christ, then ask what color they imagined, and it is statistically more likely they thought of Him as white.[7] This fact alone says so much about the prevalence of white supremacy in the Church.

But the problem is not new, as the time-capsule of Christian art reveals. It is startling to walk through a religious art gallery and suddenly wake up to the fact that every depiction of God or Jesus is blatantly and unashamedly white. Why is a white representation of God considered the norm, but whenever there is a black or olive depiction of Jesus, it is too political? That was the case with Ronald Harrison's controversial painting of a black Jesus hanging on the cross with white soldiers around him. Harrison painted this work following the Sharpeville Massacre in South Africa, the largest protest against apartheid. All of a sudden we care about the color of God when it is the color of the oppressed—to this day Harrison's painting is considered "blasphemous"—but when God is artistically identified with the oppressor, such as the popular white "Head of Christ" by Warner Sallman, we are silent. Why is Sallman's Christ the most recognizable image of Jesus, while Harrison's more profound portrayal has been condemned as blasphemy and largely forgotten? Only in a world that deems white "normal" and black "abnormal" could the middle-eastern, poverty-stricken Jesus of Nazareth be transformed into an American, middle-class white man with little dissent.

As the "image of the invisible God," our definition of God is intimately connected with how we think of Jesus Christ. Even if we rationally understand that such depictions are artistic and symbolic, they still matter because they say so much about the unspoken conclusions influencing our doctrine of God. We assume that a white God is "neutral" and a black God too political. But this is again the error of white privilege, which believes whiteness is objective and universal while blackness is subjective and limited. But the only thing a white God means is that white supremacy is the ideological core of our doctrine of God. It means our God is the God of the oppressors, but that is heresy. The Bible provides a plethora of examples to show God's identification with the poor and weak against the wealthy and powerful. God is the God of the oppressed.

While no theologian would say God is physically white or black, representation still matters in exploring our unspoken assumptions about whose side God is on. Art depicting a white God is merely the expression of our subconscious identification of God with the concerns of white, powerful, rich men—that God is on their side. But the God revealed in Christ challenges this assumption by identifying God not with the powerful and rich, but with the weak, poor, and oppressed.

The God of the Bible

The exodus and exile of Israel are foundational to the declaration that God is black. Cone writes, "God's election of oppressed Israelites has unavoidable implications for the doing of theology. [...] Here God discloses that he is the God of history whose will is identical with the liberation of the oppressed from social and political bondage."[8] The God of Israel is the God who joins the plight of the oppressed and makes their history and struggle for liberation God's own. God identified unreservedly with the plight of enslaved Israelites, as even the Ten Commandments reveal: "I am the Lord your God, who brought you out of the land of Egypt, out of the house of slavery; you shall have no other gods before me" (Exodus 20:2-3). God chiefly defined Godself to the Israelites as their historical liberator.

In the New Testament, Christ is the culmination of God's identification with oppressed Israelites. In a stunning act of divine humiliation, God condescended to an oppressed people. It is foolish to ignore the implications of God becoming a *Jewish* man under the oppressive Roman Empire. Christ lived in extreme poverty for most of His life. He was condemned by the elites as a revolutionary zealot, and the enforcers of state power killed Him as a political scapegoat.

Yet despite the Bible's political definition of God, white theology has played theological bomb-squad; they have tirelessly worked to defuse the revolutionary potential of Christ's identification with the poor and oppressed. We must reclaim a radical vision of God's political preference for the least of these. White theology has compartmentalized Christ's life and death into purely spiritual or moral categories. Thus, white theology is the heresy of political docetism, the denial of Christ's humanity, including the social, political, and material implications of His life.

Cone is concerned with arriving at a more *Biblical* understanding of God according to God's acts in the history of liberation. God is black because God was and is the God of Israel; God is black because God is the Father of Jesus Christ.

God actively participates in the history of the oppressed. In Christ, that history was expanded from its exclusive focus on the Jewish people to include all the marginalized and poor throughout the world. That means God identifies with the black struggle for liberation. Black is the color of oppression in the world today. That is true for black bodies brutalized by the streets and prisons of America and black societies throughout the third-world exploited by the white first-world. God is black means that God is on the side of oppressed people everywhere.

That may seem like it contradicts the notion of a God who is universally for everybody, who loves all people, but we have to make a careful distinction. God loves everyone, yes, but God does not take everyone's side equally. Think it through. Was God on the side of the Nazis? Is God on the side of the Klu Klux Klan? God may love everyone, but God certainly takes sides in the struggle for justice. A neutral God cannot be a righteous God. God is not equally for right and wrong, evil and good; God takes sides. The Scriptures are clear about this, too. God was not on the side of the Egyptians but made a clear stand for the liberation of the Israelites. So today, God takes sides with the oppressed, poor, and black. God's commitment to justice excludes the notion of an apathetic God.

The theme of liberation is central to the Bible, even though white theology has neglected its importance. Cone directly experienced this strange contradiction as his teachers professed God's solidarity with the oppressed historically while denying it in the present. He recalls:

> [A]lmost every biblical and theological teacher I had encountered in graduate school, as well as most of the well-known biblical scholars I read, claimed that revelation was not an abstract propositional truth but rather a historical event, God's involvement in history. [...] We black theologians contended that if God sided with the poor and the weak in biblical times, then why not today? If salvation is a historical event of rescue, a deliverance of slaves from Egypt, why not a black power event today and a deliverance of blacks from white American racial oppression? 9

Cone's central thesis that the Scriptures are about God's involvement in the history of liberation is not at odds with biblical scholarship. He cites well-respected figures such as Ernest G. Wright, Oscar Cullmann, and Gerhard von Rad. Cone takes revelation-in-history too seriously to let it become another abstract idea with no bearing on the present struggles for liberation. If the God of the Bible identified with the struggles of the oppressed, then God is involved still today in the fight for justice. The same God who identified with the plight of the Israelites and became a man in Jesus Christ is the God we worship and serve today.

Philosophical God vs. the God of history

The doctrine of God is too important to remain trapped in the world of abstract thought. God is not a mere philosophical principle or an absolute first cause. God is the God of historical liberation who acts on behalf of the oppressed. Wherever there is oppression, God is present and stands in solidarity with the least of these. It is not enough to see God abstractly as the God who liberates the captives in some purely spiritual sense; we must go further and see God among materially and physically oppressed people here and now.

"The central theme of biblical religion is the justice of God," writes Cone. "Yahweh is known by what he does in history, and what he does is always identical with the liberation of the poor from the injustice of the strong."10 God reveals Godself by acting in history. This method is in sharp contrast with the speculative, philosophical approach to knowing God. As noted in the previous chapter, Cone follows Barth's actualism by stressing God's self-revelation in history, the unity of God's being and act. Because God reveals Godself through the act of liberation in Jesus Christ, God defines Godself as the God of the oppressed. God's identity is not a static category; rather, it is the dynamic event of God's involvement in history.

As Cone and Wilmore argue, God's identity is bound to the history of liberation:

> The biblical God is the God who is involved in the historical process for the purpose of human liberation. To know him is to know what he is doing in historical events as they relate to the liberation of the oppressed. [...] To know God, therefore, is to know the actuality of oppression and the certainty of liberation.[11]

God's self-revelation takes place in the confines of historical reality, not in a vacuum. Thus, God is necessarily involved in the liberation struggles of poor and powerless people against the bondage of oppression. To ignore God's self-identification in favor of a politically neutral, theologically abstract God, is to fall short of the Gospel entirely. God is not just symbolically the God of the oppressed; God truly takes on the status of the oppressed. It is not hyperbole when the Bible declares, "Whoever oppresses the poor insults his maker" (Proverbs 14:21). God has bound Godself to the plight of the weak, powerless, poor, forsaken, and oppressed. An offense against the least of these is an offense against God.

Cone has brilliantly shifted the doctrine of God away from the realm of abstract speculation, in which theology has little bearing on ethics or praxis. He refused to separate who God is in Godself from God's being-for-us. Theology and praxis are so intertwined that we cannot speak of God abstractly without being compelled theologically to act by fighting to overthrow the oppression that God suffers together with the oppressed. Our Christian identity is thus bound to our involvement in the liberation struggle. We must be allies of black liberation. Christ is not found in a sterile Church but on the streets with the oppressed, fighting for justice. If we are Christians, then we will be found where Christ is. If God is black with the oppressed in America and the third-world, then we must become black with God.

Symbolic blackness

When Cone argues that God is black, he does not mean *literal, physiological* blackness. He uses the term in a symbolic sense by distinguishing between ontological and physiological blackness.[12] As Singleton explains:

> Cone distinguishes between a physiological blackness and an ontological blackness. The former refers to black people in America who have been the victims of white racist hegemony. And because of this, Black Theology sees them as the sole source of revelation in the world. In so being, Christian theology, for Cone, cannot speak of God without departing from the black experience in America. The latter is an ontological symbol for all people who participate in the liberation of humanity from oppression. Thus, physiological blackness represents the particular dimension of Black Theology while ontological blackness represents its universal dimension.[13]

God may not have a literal color, but God has always had a symbolic one. White theology hides behind the illusion of color-blindness and feigns political neutrality, but that is, in effect, no different than supporting white supremacy directly by allowing its injustices to go on unchallenged. The symbol of God's color may seem theologically irrelevant, but it reveals so much about the Church's relation to oppression. We must rethink how we symbolize God, but more importantly, we must rethink our uncritical acceptance of an oppressive status quo.

Cone explains:

> When I said that Jesus is black and God is black, white theologians were outraged and thought I lost my theological sanity. But it was my way of saying that Jesus was a Jew and God was identified with the oppressed. This is not a literal statement about skin color. It is [...] not a statement about biology. It is a symbolic, poetic statement about God, like saying Jesus is a rock in a weary land, the lily of the valley, and the bright morning star. [...] Theological talk about God is symbolic.[14]

To be the Church of Jesus Christ, we must take sides against white supremacy and become black with God, finding our identity in solidarity with the poor and oppressed. It is an ontological position, not necessarily a physical one. Neutrality is violence against the poor and weak, and to make God neutral is thus to make God guilty of that same violence.

White theology seldom affirms God's whiteness explicitly. It is more often through subtle allegiances, which nonetheless symbolically assert whiteness. White theology often does this by identifying God's will with the will of those in power, usually in the name of "law and order." Thus, they implicitly declare that Christian ethics are identical with the laws enacted by the state, that obedience to state power is a Christian virtue. But in reality, whenever the laws and systems of society are unjust, Christians are obligated to overthrow them by whatever means necessary.

Consider one of the most visible signs of white supremacy: the prison-industrial complex. By affirming this systemic policy, white theology reinforces the doctrine of God's whiteness, i.e., God's affirmation of an oppressive status quo. Angela Davis helpfully clarifies what the "prison-industrial complex" means. The phrase aims to

> contest prevailing beliefs that increased levels of crime were the root cause of mounting prison populations. Instead, [...] prison construction and the attendant drive to fill these new structures with human bodies have been driven by ideologies of racism and the pursuit of profit.[15]

Thus, the term refers to the idea that prisons are not built to solve a rising crime problem, but the opposite: the crime problem is fabricated to increase the profitability of prisons. The motivation is apparent when you study the rise of private, for-profit prisons and the frequent use of cheap prison labor by hundreds if not thousands of companies. Prison labor is slavery by another name, as Douglas A. Blackmon argued.[16] The 13th amendment did not abolish slavery; rather, it relocated it from the cotton fields to the jail cells.[17]

Thus, as Davis explains, prisons are racist institutions, "Racism provides the fuel for maintenance, reproduction, and expansion of the prison-industrial complex."[18] The current system of policing and sentencing in America is verifiably racist towards black and brown people, and it is also cruel towards the poor and powerless.[19] America has the largest prison population globally, which is disproportionally filled with persons of color. If we are going to take an antiracist stand against white supremacy, we must abolish prisons and the police. But white theology has aligned God with American power so often that it refuses to accept the possibility that God might be for prison abolition or at least against mass incarceration. The idea may seem too radical, but we should remember that abolishing slavery was also once considered an extreme position. Christianity has become anti-revolutionary, but we should recapture the spirit of radical hope in the coming Kingdom exemplified by the early Christians. We lack the imagination to hope for a world beyond prisons and the police, a world of justice and equality in which criminals are rehabilitated rather than violently robbed of their humanity. The white Church fails to imagine such a world because it has aligned itself with unjust power structures. But God is on the side of the under-class, the prisoner, and the poor, not on the side of those in power who support the status quo because they benefit from its injustices.

The suggestion to abolish prisons is not as radical as it may appear and involves a deeper restructuring of society. We must be willing to ask: Why have prisons replaced mental health services, affordable housing, drug rehabilitation facilities, and poverty-aid programs? American prisons house the people society has failed. As Davis explains, prisons function "ideologically as an abstract site which undesirables are deposited, relieving us of the responsibility of thinking about the real issues afflicting those communities from which prisoners are drawn in such dispropor-tionate numbers."[20] Is there a better way to deal with prisoners? Would it not be better for society as a whole if we addressed the root cause of crimi-nality—such as poverty, the debt crisis, the war on drugs, capitalism, racism, and sexism—rather than criminalizing the downtrodden by locking them in cages?

The prison-industrial complex speaks volumes about our priorities. We see criminals as sub-human creatures to be controlled, abused, and exploited rather than human beings made in the image of God worthy of dignity and respect. We act violently towards those on the margins of society rather than treating them with the proper care that every human being deserves. Yet God is in their midst, and our systemic mistreatment of the poor, weak, and incarcerated is a perpetual sin against God. White theology is guilty whenever it silently allows the injustices of the current prison system to go on unchallenged. To overcome racism, capitalism, sexism, and to eliminate America's unjust cruelty against the poor, mentally ill, and drug-dependent means abolishing prisons and imagining a world beyond the brutality of "an eye for an eye" justice. Christ proclaimed liberty to the captives and freedom to the prisoners (Luke 4:18). At the very least, that should cause us to reconsider our silent acceptance of America's prison-industrial complex.[21]

White theology has subtly reinforced the doctrine of a white God who stands on the side of the status quo by preaching allegiance to the white supremacy of our current legal system, especially its uncritical loyalty to police officers and prisons. By placing God on the side of the police who racially profile and violently abuse black men and women or prisons that systemically disenfranchise the black, brown, and poor, white theology colors God white. It is a question of power. Is God on the side of the powerful oppressor or the powerless oppressed? Is God on the side of the violent systems of inhumanity or of its victims? White theology places God on the side of the oppressor, symbolically coloring God white whenever it aligns God's will with the will of state powers and systems. Prisons and the police are just two examples of state powers uncritically accepted by white theology. The military-industrial complex is another example. But by silently adopting an uncritical attitude towards these systems, white Christians are just as guilty of racism as the racist systems they support.

Another notable example of white theology's complicity in oppression is the prevalence of the prosperity Gospel in the American Church. It is common for Christians to accept this unholy alliance of Western capitalist values and Christian faith, even though capitalism is an oppressive system that prioritizes profits over people.[22] The idolatry of Mammon found in capitalism cannot co-exist with Christian devotion to the God of Jesus Christ, who declared, "You cannot serve God and wealth [Mammon]" (Matthew 6:24). God takes sides with the poor against the rich, yet white Christianity has become a religion that coddles the rich and oppresses the poor. Whenever the Church fails to challenge the oppressive status quo by siding with the rich and powerful, it has given itself over to the idol of a white God.

The blackness of God is an ontological declaration of God's solidarity with oppressed people everywhere. It is sinful and misguided to place God on the side of the oppressor. Yet white theology has ontologically situated God on the side of the rich and powerful, coloring God white even if they have not explicitly made the connection. Uncritically accepting the power structures of white supremacy that keep men and women in bondage means identifying God as the God of the oppressor, the God of Herod, and not of Jesus Christ.

Whenever those in power claim to have God on their side, the unthinkable becomes justifiable. That was Barth's concern when he rejected liberal theology. He refused to accept a theology that endorsed state power and identified it with the will of God. Today, the Christian church should be skeptical of any state power that claims God as their own. As Bob Dylan's "With God On Our Side" warns: "And you never ask questions / when God's on your side." Our God identifies with the poor and weak, those on the margins of society rather than those in power. Thus, we should always be ready to challenge the status quo in the name of Jesus Christ, in the name of the excluded and oppressed. If Jesus is the image of the invisible God, then part of His Gospel message includes the destruction of our idols. Cone vehemently rejects the white racist's God in the name of Jesus Christ. God is on the side of the powerless.

Jesus was not born into Herod's court, nor was he a friend of the rich and powerful. He stood *against* those in power, frequently criticized the rich, and died as a scapegoat to appease political powers. Christ's poverty and moralistic stance against the rich reveal a God unequivocally against limitless accumulations of wealth. God is on the side of the powerless in society. God in Christ declares radical solidarity with the least of these, with the oppressed, the poor, and the downtrodden.

The poet Hölderlin wrote, "Near is God, and difficult to grasp." It is *because* God is near to humanity that God is so hard to grasp. God is not hiding away in the heavens. Barthian theology is correct to affirm the non-objectifiability of God, God's quantitative distinction from humanity. Yet, it is easy to overemphasize God's transcendence so much that we miss God's immanent self-abasement and radical solidarity with the weak and poor. God is not an object we might grasp and control, but God identifies with the least of these. It is often easier to talk about a universal God who loves everyone, a God somewhere "out there," but it gets hard to talk about God when we see God's face in the poor and oppressed among us. Kendrick Lamar's chillingly prophetic song "How Much a Dollar Cost" is an excellent example of God's identification with the poor and oppressed. Lamar's paradoxical faith is more profound, if less polished, than the cheap sentiments of white theology.

A color-blind doctrine of God is heresy. God takes sides. We must *Christianize* our doctrine of God. Still today, we must see God on the side of the powerless, poor, weak, and black. God is hard to grasp because God is so near. God identifies Godself with the homeless beggars on our city streets, with the poor men and women struggling in the black-ghettos and forgotten slums, with the marginalized people thrown in prisons and jails, and with all the powerless people of the world. God is the color of the oppressed.

Love and justice

God's love is incomplete without justice. It is shallow to see the problem of racism in America today and say all we need is more love. Love is not a cheap, sentimental "let's come together, hold hands, and sing by the campfire" kind of love. Love demands justice for the wronged. It requires the destruction of all systems of oppression and the liberation of the captives from their bondage. When white liberals adopt the attitude that "love is all you need," it is often to ignore the larger issues of justice and liberation. It is an attempt to do something about their guilt but not the underlying causes of injustice. Yet racism and white supremacy are festering wounds. To ignore the systemic injustices in favor of bandaid solutions is the height of hypocritical ignorance. As Cone writes, "Justice-loving people must never stop getting mad at oppression."[23] May we never confuse love with cheap peace. Love costs something, it demands justice, and it often looks like passionate anger. God's love in the face of injustice looks like boiling wrath; so should ours. If we do not get angry at oppression, it will never cease. If our God is indifferent to oppression, then our God is not a God of justice.

White liberals love to praise Martin Luther King, Jr., as the prime example of Christian love and activism. But we have romanticized his legacy. As Cone has shown, King would have been just as critical of white Christians today as he was then. How quickly we forget that King was, at one time, the most hated man in America. King criticized the "white moderates" who call for peace without justice, and he even considered them "more of a stumbling block" to black liberation than the KKK.[24] Theologically, the idea that God is color-blind and colorless robs God's love of its radical commitment to justice. A color-blind God is a God blind to right and wrong, justice and injustice.

Cone writes:

> Black theology will accept only a love of God which participates in the destruction of the white oppressor. With Fanon, black theology takes literally Jesus' statement, 'the last will be first, and the first last.' Black power 'is the putting into practice of this sentence.' [...] God's love and God's righteousness are two ways of talking about the same reality.

Righteousness means that God is addressing the black condition; love means God is doing so in the interests of both blacks and whites. The blackness of God points to the righteousness of God, as well as to the love of God.[25]

It is essential to affirm the blackness of God. It is a statement of God's commitment to justice, of making right the wrongs of history. If we do not affirm God's ontological blackness, then the God we profess is not the God of the Bible: "But let justice roll down like waters, and righteousness like an ever-flowing stream" (Amos 5:24). To say that God is black is to say that God is committed to love and justice, that God is on the side of the poor and oppressed. Any other God is a demonic idol that stands by silently in the face of oppression. Our God takes sides; God is black.

3

THE GOSPEL OF LIBERATION

Summary: The Gospel of Jesus Christ is revolutionary; it is a scandalous message of condemnation to the rich and powerful, yet it is a joyous message of liberty to the poor and weak. Spiritual salvation is incomplete without material and political liberation. Christology must lead to Christopraxis; knowing Christ means following Him into solidarity with the least of these. The lynching tree is America's cross, and Christ is re-crucified still today in the lynching of black and brown bodies.

In Cone's words:

> Jesus is not safely confined in the first century. He is our contemporary, proclaiming release to the captives and rebelling against all who silently accept the structures of injustice. If he is not in the ghetto, if he is not where men are living at the brink of existence, but is, rather, in the easy life of the suburbs, then the gospel is a lie. The opposite, however, is the case. Christianity is not alien to Black Power; it is Black Power.[1]

> The lynching tree is America's cross. [...] If we want to understand what the crucifixion means for Americans today, we must view it through the lens of mutilated black bodies whose lives are destroyed in the criminal justice system. Jesus continues to be lynched before our eyes. He is

crucified wherever people are tormented. That is why I say Christ is black.[2]

Secondary quotes:

Any religion that professes to be concerned with the souls of men and is not concerned with the slums that damn them, the economic conditions that cripple them, is a spiritually moribund religion in need of new blood.[3]

— MARTIN LUTHER KING, JR.

The denunciation of injustice implies the rejection of the use of Christianity to legitimize the established order. It likewise implies, in fact, that the Church has entered into conflict with those who wield power.[4]

— GUSTAVO GUTIÉRREZ

Introduction

White theology has neutered the revolutionary significance of Christ. He has become a purely spiritual savior, with little or nothing to say to the least of these in their material and political struggles. Yet the God revealed in Christ did not come only to save souls but also liberate captives and preach good news to the poor. Salvation necessarily includes material liberation from the bondage of oppression.

This chapter will examine the soteriological implications of Christ's solidarity with the poor and oppressed. Christ proclaimed a coming kingdom, not a heavenly escape. His message embraces the history of the oppressed, and it proclaims hope for their liberation. As Cone writes, "If God came to us in the human presence of Jesus, then no theology can transcend the material conditions of humanity and still retain its Christian identity."[5] The humanity of Christ necessitates that we expand our vision of salvation to include historical liberation from social, political, and economic bondage. Accordingly, Cone urges the Church to reject the eschatology of escapism.

Jesus the Israelite

James Cone challenges us to reconsider the political implications of Christ's Jewish identity. The incarnation signifies God's preference for the poor and weak against the rich and powerful. God did not assume neutral, white, apolitical flesh. From the start, Christ was a threat to those in power who benefit from the status quo. Herod's reaction to the news of Christ's birth was a clear indication of how severely he felt threatened. If Christ were merely a spiritual revolutionary, as white theology implies, Herod would have no reason to react the way he did. But Herod panicked because Christ was and is still a political threat to every power that establishes itself by oppressing and marginalizing the least of these. Luke's account highlights this further by defining Christ's public ministry with an unmistakably political pronouncement from Isaiah:

> The Spirit of the Lord is upon me, because he has anointed me to bring good news to the poor. He has sent me to proclaim release to the captives and recovery of sight to the blind, to let the oppressed go free, to proclaim the year of the Lord's favor.[6]

The Gospel is a stumbling block for all who define themselves by their privileged status in society. How else would we explain Christ's difficult words: "Truly I tell you, it will be hard for a rich person to enter the kingdom of heaven. Again I tell you, it is easier for a camel to go through the eye of a needle than for someone who is rich to enter the kingdom of God" (Matthew 19:23-4). Christ's message is bad news for the powerful, wealthy, white oppressors, but it is good news for the powerless and oppressed. Those with power must renounce it, and those with wealth must give it away. "So the last will be first, and the first will be last" (Matthew 20:16). The Gospel is a radical, revolutionary challenge to the status quo; anything less is a distortion of Christ's mission and message.

If we ignore the political facets of Christ's life and teachings and focus solely on a spiritualized doctrine of salvation, we affirm the heresy of docetism. That is, we deny the humanity of Christ in practice. Few white theologians would adopt a docetic Christology, but white theology affirms political docetism by ignoring the physical and economic needs of the oppressed. Cone echoes this point, "His presence with the poor today is not docetic; but like yesterday, today also he takes the pain of the poor upon himself and bears it for them."[7] Jesus Christ is still among the poor and needy. To ignore the plight of the least of these is to deny Christ's presence in their midst. It is to deny the incarnation, the truth that Christ stands in solidarity with the oppressed by taking up their poverty and marginalization. Christ's humanity is God's unwavering identification with the least of these, the pronouncement that God is the God of the oppressed.

Cone affirms, accordingly, the declaration that Jesus Christ is black, and explains: "He *is* black because he *was* a Jew."[8] If we want to know where Christ is today, we should ask where He was in the first century. The Bible bears witness to His presence among the poor, oppressed, powerless, and excluded; thus, Christ is black, the color of oppression in our midst. As Cone writes, "The 'blackness of Christ,' therefore, is not simply a statement about skin color, but rather, the transcendent affirmation that God has not ever, no not ever, left the oppressed alone in struggle."[9]

What we must begin to realize is that Christ's message was not purely spiritual. Because Jesus historically identified with the struggle of oppressed Israelites, the Gospel today must involve the physical, historical liberation of the poor. The Gospel is good news for the whole person, not just our spiritual existence, as Cone writes:

> [L]iberation theology in all forms rejects the dichotomy between spiritual and physical salvation, between faith and political praxis, and insists on their dialectical relationship. [...] This means that the gospel is inseparably connected with the bodily liberation of the poor.[10]

Jesus' Jewish identity must be for us a continual reminder that God has bound Godself to the struggle of oppressed people everywhere. Because Christ identified with the plight of that particular people in their struggle for liberation, the Gospel must include the material liberation of the oppressed. God is not spiritually aloof from history or indifferent to the plight of the poor, but in Christ, God takes up the struggle for justice in history. A Christology that ignores the political imperatives of the Gospel fails to witness to Jesus of Nazareth faithfully.

Bodily liberation vs. escapism

White theology has turned the Gospel into a message of escape, not liberation. But our Christian hope is in the transformation of *this* world, the coming of God's Kingdom on Earth as it is in heaven. Our hope is for the bodily liberation of oppressed people.

Consider, as an example, the evangelical obsession with "end times," particularly its uncritical acceptance of the rapture theory. This fixation on eschatological theories, often to the point of creating wild interpretations of current events based on a poor understanding of Revelation, only goes to show the prevalence of escapism in their understanding of the Gospel. I grew up in this sort of environment, as I wrote in my early, though flawed, little book, *10 Reasons Why the Rapture Must Be Left Behind* (2015). I know well the paranoia of escapism and how it distorts one's perception of world events because I lived it for years.

I remember one frightful, tear-soaked evening as a young boy, staying up all night because I firmly believed Christ would come back, and fearing that if I slept, I would miss Him. I walked around school the next day in a daze, thinking to myself, "This shouldn't be here, the world was supposed to end last night." That may be an extreme example, but white, evangelical theology nonetheless has, at its core, an ideological commitment to escapism. The rapture theory is the most obvious sign of this. For white theology, because of its commitment to end times, the material concerns of the poor are shrugged off and disregarded, justice becomes less of a priority than reading the signs of the times, and it all comes at the cost of neglecting the least of these for a widely debunked reading of apocalyptic texts.

So it should be no surprise that white theology rejects Cone's commitment to justice and liberation here-and-now, even calling it heretical to focus on social justice. They have traded Christ's Gospel of liberation for a fear-based message of destruction and escape, of spiritual salvation. For white theology, the Gospel is about going to heaven when we die, of fleeing our material and bodily world for an ethereal existence, rather than Christ's message of Kingdom come. Christ entered our world in all its material, physical conditions, but they want to escape it.[11]

Our hope is in the coming Kingdom of God, and so we fight today to usher in the reign of God's justice here and now. As Jürgen Moltmann writes, "Those who hope in Christ can no longer put up with reality as it is, but begin to suffer under it, to contradict it."[12] In the certainty of resurrection hope, we fight against injustice in the name of Christ. Our discontentment with the state of this world goads us into revolutionary action, not escapism.

Cone writes:

An eschatological perspective that does not challenge the present order is faulty. If contemplation about the future distorts the present reality of injustice and reconciles the oppressed to unjust treatment committed against them, then it is unchristian and thus has nothing whatsoever to do with the Christ who came to liberate us.[13]

White theology fails to be Christian theology whenever its message to oppressed people is to accept their unjust condition. This complacency with the status quo leads to a denial of the Gospel, which was never about getting into heaven but of doing God's will on Earth as it is in heaven. Our definition of salvation must be expanded to include the liberation of the oppressed, meeting the material needs of the poor and caring for the bodily health of the sick. Thus, the Gospel must be politically concerned with the least of these.

For Cone, salvation is "grounded in history," and "there is no way to separate the preaching of the gospel from a political commitment on behalf of the oppressed of the land."[14] Political concern for the weak and powerless is not an auxiliary duty of the Christian faith; it *is* the Gospel. Christ's proclamation liberates the oppressed to overthrow their oppression. As Cone explained in one of his best attempts at defining the Gospel:

> The Christian gospel is God's good news to the victims that their humanity is not determined by their victimization. This means that the poor do not have to adjust to poverty; the oppressed do not have to reconcile themselves to humiliation and suffering. They can do something to change not only their perception of themselves, but also the existing structures of oppression.[15]

This definition gets right to the heart of what makes Cone's theology so unique, especially in contrast with white theology's apolitical escapism. The danger of a Gospel that focuses so exclusively on the hope of escaping to salvation *in another world* is that it turns the Christian faith into an "opium of the people," as Marx criticized. Indeed, if the Christian Gospel promises liberation only in death, salvation *from* the body, then it is rightly condemned by Marx. But for Cone, the Gospel means God's solidarity with our revolutionary struggle against the systems of injustice and oppression. It proclaims the good news that our struggle is *God's* struggle, that justice belongs to the Lord. God is a God of justice and fights with us in our efforts for liberation. In the death and resurrection of Christ, there is freedom from the bondage of oppression, and so, whenever we fight against injustice, we do it in the name of God and with the firm hope that the same God who raised Jesus from the dead is with us in our struggles.

The Gospel is a message of political and social revolution. Yet those in power have done everything they can to turn it into a message of escape and complacency, of purely spiritual liberation. If the Church is to be Christ's Church, then we must follow His example and become a constant threat against the status quo and those who uphold it, rather than making accommodations with systemic oppression.

While Cone focuses on the poor and oppressed's material and political liberation, it is essential to note that he does not wholly neglect the spiritual implications of the Gospel. That is a common misunderstanding about liberation theology. Because white theology focuses so singularly on spiritual salvation, Cone's emphasis on liberation here-and-now feels like a betrayal of the Gospel. But it is not either-or. *Because* we hope for a new heaven and a new Earth, we work tirelessly for the liberation of the oppressed.

Cone hopes for liberation in history but also beyond history, the transcendent element of our faith. Indeed, "You can't resist unless you hope."[16] For Cone, this hope is the most radical dimension of the New Testament. Yet he aims to focus our attention on the political aspects of the Gospel, even and especially as it relates to the plight of the oppressed. The two concerns are not at odds but are necessary allies. We hope for life in the world to come, and that hope goads us into direct action for the sake of the least of these in our midst.

The Christian faith, rather than opium for the masses, is a rallying cry to fight against oppression and injustice. The death and resurrection of Christ are central to this cry. Cone explains the dual importance of hoping for the future and thus being unreconciled to the present:

> The New Testament, while accepting history, does not limit salvation to history. As long as people are bound to history, they are bound to law and thus death. [...] But if the oppressed, while living in history, can see beyond it, if they can visualize an eschatological future beyond this world, then the 'sigh of oppressed creatures,' to use Marx's phrase, can become a revolutionary cry of rebellion against the established order. It is this revolutionary cry that is granted in the resurrection of Jesus. Salvation then is not simply freedom in history; it is freedom to affirm

that future which is beyond history. [...] The transcendence-factor in salvation helps us to realize that our fight against justice is God's fight too; and his presence in Jesus' resurrection has already defined what the ultimate outcome will be.[17]

Because of Christ's victory over sin and death, we fight tirelessly to transform this world into the Kingdom of God. On the strength of our certainty that the fight will succeed—because it is not our struggle alone but also *God's*—we work with joy and courage for a beautiful future. If our definition of salvation does not consider the material, social, political, *and* spiritual needs of humanity, it is not the Gospel Christ proclaimed.

A revolutionary Gospel

The Gospel is a revolutionary call to change the world, not escape it. White theology, by over-spiritualizing Christ's message, has distorted the revolutionary imperatives of Christian faith. It has used Christ's life and teachings to legitimize the established order rather than being a continual threat to the powers of empire. We have exchanged a theology of Kingdom come for a powerless Gospel in service of supporting the status quo, doing nothing in the face of injustice, and hiding away in the ignorant bliss of spiritual escapism. We have traded Christ's call for revolutionary change for a message of behavioral modification. Christianity has deteriorated into a game of who can perform better and occasionally convert their friends to profess the same creed while ignoring the ongoing injustices around us.

This problem stems from the depoliticization of the Christian faith. Rather than seeing the connection between Christ's message and the fight for political liberation, white theology has resigned itself to an individualistic interpretation of salvation. But Christ's Gospel is a call to change the world, not merely the individual. Salvation must be social and political. That is why white theology's Gospel fails to confront the oppressive systems of white supremacy, and instead, often lends its support to the injustices of the established order. In other words, white theology preaches a different Gospel, an anti-revolutionary message of a private faith that accepts and never confronts the status quo.

Conservative politicians have been especially eager to exploit the anti-revolutionary inclinations of an overly-spiritualized, privatized Gospel. But the political alliance of Christianity with right-wing ideology—particularly the idols of imperialism, capitalism, militarism, and nationalism—is a heresy against the message of Jesus Christ. Republicans frequently support policies that actively harm the poor, foreign, black, and marginalized. In other words, they actively support the oppression of the least of these, those whom Christ called His own. James Cone's voice is a much-needed wake-up call for the Church to renounce its allegiance to the powers that be. An oppressive political structure murdered Jesus, and the right-wing Church makes its bed with these same powers today.

This is not to imply that the liberal Church is any better. In many ways, as Malcolm X warned, the liberal is more dangerous than the conservative. Dr. King minced no words in calling white moderates a greater threat to black liberation than even the most ardent racists. He wrote from a Birmingham jail, "The Negro's great stumbling block in his stride toward freedom is not the White Citizen's Councilor or the Ku Klux Klanner, but the white moderate, who is more devoted to 'order' than to justice."[18] Striving to maintain peace without first achieving justice only furthers oppression. Liberal Democrats love to appear progressive by offering token gestures, but they do little to help the poor and oppressed concretely. Joining a protest or posting something on social media is a nice idea, but if it does not work towards tangible changes in policy, it is no more than an empty gesture. Performance-based (rather than results-based) activism is a white-guilt management technique disguised as progress.

Token gestures are not enough; the time is now for overthrowing all systems of oppression by any means necessary, even if it comes at the cost of white people giving up their privileged, comfortable status in society. White liberals love to be allies in social revolutions right up until it begins to cost them something. They get angry at police brutality and racism but stop short of being radicalized by that anger. It is anger as a fad, not as a revolution. Liberals fail to let their frustrations goad them into educating themselves, listening to black stories, reading theory, renouncing their complicity in systemic racism, and fighting for a better world. Most of all, we must change the policies and structures of oppression, not merely speaking out in protest but enacting change. The token gestures of liberal Democrats are substantially no better than blatant racism in this regard. They fail to see the underlining causes of injustice and strive for bandaid solutions over systemic change. Only when we are more concerned with overthrowing the policies and structures of oppression, judging our success on this alone, will white liberals be real allies in the fight for black liberation.

A Gospel that confronts no one comforts no one. The Gospel goes beyond the cheap ideologies of any political party used to reinforce the status quo, whether Republican or Democrat; rather, the Gospel is a message of the poor for their liberation, a revolutionary call to political change. Status quo Christianity has domesticated the liberating power of Jesus Christ, but we must rediscover His revolutionary significance. Christ's Gospel is *against* the rich and *for* the poor, *against* white supremacy and *for* black liberation, and *against* oppressors and *for* the oppressed. It confronts to comfort. We must take a stand against injustice for Christ's sake. To preach any other Gospel is to deny Christ. Cone powerfully writes:

> Christians must fight against evil, for not to fight, not to do everything they can for their neighbor's pain, is to deny the resurrection.[19]

What good is Christology without Christopraxis? Is it enough to know *about* Christ without following *the way* of Jesus? What use is profound theological insight if it does not drastically affect the way we live? It is not enough to profess Jesus. We must also follow Him into solidarity with the least of these, fight for liberation, and confront status quo complacency, even and especially the complacency in our hearts. That means we must be antiracist, actively fighting against systemic racism in our world. And we must be anti-capitalist, actively fighting against the systemic exploitation of the poor. We must be starkly opposed to all forms of injustice, taking the time to analyze the causes of oppression and then to let our analysis lead to praxis. The Gospel calls us to fight for revolutionary change.

We deny the resurrection in practice whenever we deny God's power to liberate the oppressed here and now. We reject the resurrection whenever we ignore the political imperatives articulated by Christ's identification with an oppressed people. We deny the resurrection whenever we turn our back on His presence in the least of these. Christ is homeless on our streets, a stranger at our borders, alone and hopeless in our prisons, exploited in the third world, and black amid systemic racism. We forsake Christ whenever we forsake the poor and oppressed. If we do not act for the sake of the oppressed in the name of Christ, then I question whether we have known Christ at all. To know Christ is to know the least of these.

Christopraxis follows Christology; a new vision of Christ demands a new ethical call to action. As the body of Christ, the Church is not at home in a white, middle-class, suburban neighborhood that ignores rampant injustice, but in the ghettos, the slums, and the poverty of the third world. Where is Christ today? Where is His Kingdom? He is with the black bodies that suffer from economic apartheid in the ghettos of America. He is with the third world people who have been raped and exploited by the imperialistic first world's oppressive economic powers. He is with those who cannot feed their families, who sell their labor, their youth, and their strength to make the rich richer. He is with the handicap and the sick. He is with the homeless. He is always—always—with the least of these.

If we are Christ's Church, we must follow Him into solidarity with the poor, weak, underprivileged, black, and oppressed. Christ is today among beggars and prostitutes, not politicians and landlords. The Church must also be the people of Christ's body by joining the poor and oppressed in their struggle, fighting side by side for the liberation of all humanity. In Cone's words, we must "become black" with Christ, bearing the color of oppression symbolically through the way we live. Then and only then will the Church be more than a social club of like-minded, middle-class, apolitical people. We will be Kingdom people.

The Gospel is bad news to oppressors

Justice for the oppressed means judgment for their oppressors. As Cone writes, "The gospel of liberation is *bad news* to all oppressors, because they have defined their 'freedom' in terms of the slavery of others."[20] God must be *against* oppressors to be *for* the oppressed. Yet it is not an absolute opposition. God is *for* oppressors by being *against* their status as oppressors, their involvement in an oppressive activity. God expresses God's concern for oppressors best by being against them. Thus, the liberation of the oppressed is at once the liberation of their oppressors from the bondage of sin. God is on the side of blackness against whiteness *for the sake of* white people.

Oppressors are just as in need of liberation as the oppressed. The difference is God's liberating activity is bad news for oppressors, a call to repentance. That means I will, as a white person, benefit from black liberation, but it will demand repentance from me, a new way of being human. It was not God's design for any individual to oppress another person or exploit them, so oppressors must be set free from their corrupt will to power. As Baldwin writes, "Whoever debases others is debasing himself."[21] But even though the Gospel liberates oppressors from their will to power, it does not excuse them from blame; they are nonetheless condemned by the Gospel, even if it is a purifying chastisement rooted in love.

The work of liberation, however, is focused on liberating the oppressed and not their oppressors because the oppressed must regain their dignity by overthrowing oppression. Liberating oppressors is never a primary goal, but rather a side-effect of liberating the oppressed. The liberation of oppressors is thus bound together with the liberation of the oppressed. Oppression is dehumanizing, and liberation must include the humanizing event of regaining one's dignity through revolutionary action. Liberation is costly. It comes at the death of the oppressor so that they might become brothers and sisters with the oppressed, no longer exploiters but friends.

Because racism is itself a kind of bondage, Cone writes, "Whites are thus enslaved to their own egos. Therefore, when blacks assert their freedom in self-determination, whites too are liberated."[22] Black liberation includes the liberation of whites from their racism and complicity in racist systems. Just as salvation means the liberation of the human being from their sin, here it means the liberation of whites from white supremacy. God is on the side of the poor, oppressed, and black because God is for all people. These two ideas do not conflict but seamlessly co-exist. God takes sides, and ultimately, God works for the good of all humanity *by* taking sides.

Jürgen Moltmann writes, "Peace is not the absence of conflict, but the presence of justice."[23] The Gospel brings conflict against the oppressors and justice for the poor. It means the death of the white oppressor and their re-birth into the struggle for liberation. The Gospel is not neutral, and neither is Jesus' liberating work on the Earth today. Christ, our liberator, takes sides *against* the oppressor *for* the freedom of the oppressed *and* the salvation of their oppressor. The Gospel is bad news for oppressors *because* it is good news for the redemption of all humanity in the freedom of God's love.

The cross and the lynching tree

Cone draws a remarkable parallel between the crucifixion of Jesus Christ for political gain under the Roman Empire and the lynching of black men and women under the American flag. America lynched thousands of black bodies in a manner strikingly similar to the Roman Empire's crucifixion method, but the comparison went unnoticed by white theology. It is paramount that we open our eyes to see this connection, as hard as it may be to face. Jesus was and is re-crucified on American soil in the brutalized bodies of lynched black men and women. The lynching tree is America's cross, and we will never understand Christ's death rightly until we understand it in the light of the lynching tree.

By connecting the cross and the lynching tree, Cone unburdens the crucifixion from its sterile pietistic and apolitical interpretations. The reality is, the cross was a dangerous, highly political, revolutionary event. Christ did not die between two candles on a beautiful alter. Christ was humiliated, brutalized, and politically shamed in a display of might and authority by the powers that be. For white America to see itself correctly, we must discover ourselves as the villains of the black experience. We must see ourselves as the Romans who crucified Christ; because when we examine our dark history of enslaving, lynching, and brutalizing black bodies, that is precisely the role we have played. We are guilty of re-crucifying Christ.

Today, lynching takes place in less obvious forms, but it is no less traumatizing to the black community. We must reject any religious interpretations of the cross as a distant event from 2,000 years ago. It takes place every day in the ghettos and slums of America. Every time the first world exploits the third world, the rich exploit the poor, or when the patriarchy oppresses women, Christ is re-crucified in the crosses of the least of these. Wherever oppressed people are abused by the powerful, Christ is re-crucified in their suffering and struggle.

The Church aligns with the same demonic forces that crucified Christ every time it has aligned itself with violent powers of oppression. There is nothing substantially different between Christ's crucifixion and how the American military terrorizes the Middle East with drones and bombs. Nor is there much difference in the way America acts towards the poor underclasses of its society. The powers that be, including white supremacy and the policies that uphold it, act with impunity still today. The Church is complicit in the re-crucifixion of Christ whenever it aligns with these sinful systems of oppression. Lynching still exists, and it is the most visible symbol of Christ's cross in our midst.

Where is Jesus Christ today? He is forsaken and alone in the prisons, suffering economic brutality in the ghettos, struggling in the oppressed third world nations, barely surviving with the poor and needy, dying with the malnourished and hungry, and dwelling in shame with the homeless. If we cannot see Christ in the least of these, we have not truly understood the Gospel. White theology has ignored God's solidarity with the oppressed because that would mean being held accountable for these injustices.

Cone brings all these points home when he writes:

> Theologically speaking, Jesus was the 'first lynchee,' who foreshadowed all the lynched black bodies on American soil. He was crucified by the same principalities and powers that lynched black people in America. Because God was present with Jesus on the cross and thereby refused to let Satan and death have the last word about his meaning, God was also present at every lynching in the United States. God saw what whites did to innocent and helpless blacks and claimed their suffering as God's own. God transformed lynched black bodies into the recrucified body of Christ. *Every time a white mob lynched a black person, they lynched Jesus.* The lynching tree is the cross in America. When American Christians realize that they can meet Jesus only in the crucified bodies in our midst, they will encounter the real scandal of the cross.[24]

The value of this perspective is immense. Cone refused to let the cross be a "magical talisman of salvation" without the power to liberate the oppressed. Instead, he aims to connect Calvary with the lynching tree and thus to de-sterilize the crucifixion event. The cross is the power of God unto salvation (Romans 1:16). Yet that is only true when it is no longer robbed of power by the sterilization of white theology. Rightly, Cone reminds us, "Until we can see the cross and the lynching tree together, until we can identify Christ with a 'recrucified' black body hanging from a lynching tree, there can be no genuine understanding of Christian iden-tity in America, and no deliverance from the brutal legacy of slavery and white supremacy."[25] We must not domesticate (de-radicalize) the scandal of the cross to fit it into our comfortable, status quo, middle-class lifestyle. The cross is an iconoclastic symbol of resistance against the status quo. America must see itself through its victims' eyes, to see the suffering of

God in the struggle for black liberation and hear God's Word in the cries of black blood throughout this land. As Cone writes:

> As I see it, the lynching tree frees the cross from the false pieties of well-meaning Christians. [...] The cross needs the lynching tree to remind Americans of the reality of suffering—to keep the cross from becoming a symbol of abstract, sentimental piety.[26]

The crucifixion is the center of Christian faith. But when our definition of the cross becomes sterile and powerless, when it fails to confront the sins of our past, it is not the same cross that crucified Christ. It is an idol of white theology. The black experience in America can help jolt Christianity out of its complacency and apathy. Without the scandal of the cross, Christianity is little more than a dead ideology, a religious game, and a social club.

The cross reveals God's solidarity with the least of these. Yet white theology has traded in God's preference for the weak and powerless for an ideological commitment to the powers of empire. But God did not save by aligning with the powerful and mighty. God saves through weakness and suffering. Every Christian should heed the powerful words Dietrich Bonhoeffer wrote from prison:

> Christ helps us not by virtue of his omnipotence but rather by virtue of his weakness and suffering! This is the crucial distinction between Christianity and all religions. Human religiosity directs people in need to the power of God in the world, God as deus ex machina. The Bible directs people toward the powerlessness and the suffering of God; only the suffering God can help.[27]

Christian faith is not the faith of the powerful and wealthy. It belongs to the abused and forgotten people of the Earth, those who live in the shadow of the cross rather than Caesar's favor. That is what makes the cross a scandal and a stumbling block. By connecting the lynching tree with the crucifixion, Cone revives the offense of the Gospel for our time. Those who are powerful, privileged, and strong are brought low and humbled by the cross, while the victimized poor and weak are exalted. For Cone, the lynching tree means that salvation is "available *only* through our solidarity with the crucified people in our midsts."[28] For America to repent and believe the Gospel, it must hear Christ's message proclaimed in the history of its violent lynching and brutality against black people. We have crucified Christ, and we crucify Him still today whenever we oppress the least of these in our midst. As Cone warns, "Just as the Germans should never forget the Holocaust, Americans should never forget slavery, segregation, and the lynching tree."[29] If we turn a blind eye to the horrors of our past, we turn away from the suffering of God in history, the re-crucifixion of Jesus with the millions of black bodies brutalized, murdered, enslaved, and oppressed still today on American soil.

When America victimizes millions of black men and women with mass incarceration, redlining, poverty, ghettoization, the death penalty, and police violence; when we rob from the poor their right to health care, an education, food, water, and adequate housing; when we terrorize third-world nations with bombs and capitalist exploitation; when we harm the least of these in our midst—America re-crucifies Christ. We must see ourselves anew through the lens of the lynching tree. Cone's work is a radical wake-up call for America to return to the scandal of the cross, to repent of all the ways we have cheapened its radical message of liberation, and to be born again to divine blackness.

May God free us from a powerless, sterile Gospel. May God strike our hearts with the realism of the crucified Christ in our midst. God's blackness means God's suffering with every brutalized black body. Jesus Christ is black! And thus, He is truly our liberator, the hope of salvation for all people to be free from the violent cycles of racism and injustice. Jesus did not remain in the first century. He is present in our midst still today as the poor and oppressed. Whenever we turn our backs on the least of these, we turn away from Christ. That is the soteriological relevance of the cross today. It is not merely the spiritual release from the bondage of sin; the cross calls us to fight against injustice, to die to ourselves, and follow the way of Christ into the struggle of the oppressed and powerless.

4

BECOMING BLACK WITH CHRIST

Summary: To be born again in an unjust society is to identify with the oppressed and share life with them as friends in solidarity, not as objects of charity. In a racist society, it is to become black with Christ. In a capitalist society, it is to become poor with the impoverished. In short, to be a disciple of Christ today means following the way of Jesus into solidarity with the least of these, making the plight and struggle of the oppressed our own. Whiteness was crucified with Christ. We must repent, take up our cross, die to whiteness, and be born again with the black Christ.

In Cone's words:

There is no place in this war of liberation for nice white people who want to avoid taking sides and remain friends with both the racists and the Negro. To hear the Word is to decide: Are you with us or against us?[1]

Being human means being against evil by joining sides with those who are the victims of evil. Quite literally, it means becoming oppressed with the oppressed, making their cause one's own cause by involving oneself in the liberation struggle. *No one is free until all are free.*[2]

Secondary quotes:

> If there is no friendship with the poor and no sharing of the life of the poor, then there is no authentic commitment to liberation, because love exists only among equals.[3]

— GUSTAVO GUTIÉRREZ

> Being in solidarity means siding with the oppressed. This means changing sides, for the truth is that the noncommitted have already adopted the side of their class or group. They need to change sides. [...] Changing sides is really more of a state of mind.[4]

— RUFUS BURROW, JR.

Introduction

One of Cone's most challenging ideas is the imperative to "become black" with Christ. It is a radical re-interpretation of Christ's call to take up the cross and follow Him, to be born again. Cone writes, "Reconciliation to God means that white people are prepared to deny themselves (whiteness), take up the cross (blackness) and follow Christ (black ghetto)."[5] How is this possible, and what does it mean? Cone clarifies, "Being black in America has very little to do with skin color. To be black means that your heart, your soul, your mind, and your body are where the dispossessed are."[6] By joining the underprivileged and oppressed throughout the world, we show that we have been reconciled to God and are black with God. This follows Cone's concept of blackness as an ontological symbol rather than a physiological skin tone, even though it is rooted in the historical reality of black people.

The Church has sterilized Christ's hard-saying that we must be born again, flippantly labeling ourselves "born again Christians." There is nothing inherently wrong with this, but when something becomes a cliché, it tends to lose its disruptive power. But initially, the call to be born again was radical and shocking. It made clear that salvation is impossible without God, that the Gospel demands a radical and complete change, not merely reform. Cone's image of becoming black with Christ retains both of these difficult conditions. In this sense, it is one of his most important contributions. The Gospel involves a total change to our existence, a complete disruption of the status quo, a new creation. To be "born again" needs to take on a fresh meaning for the Church today, and Cone's creative re-interpretation helps do exactly that.

Blackness is salvation

The Gospel calls us to repentance, to a radical change of life, identity, and status. Bonhoeffer was right when he said, "When Christ calls a man, he bids him come and die."[7] It is not enough to be a Christian nominally without also following the way of Jesus Christ. We must repent of whiteness and be born again into the Kingdom of the black Christ. But this is an act of God's grace, ultimately. Just as faith is not primarily something we do but the gift of God, so becoming black with Christ is not a work we can perform to earn salvation. Cone explains:

> The question 'How can white persons become black?' is analogous to the Philippian Jailer's question to Paul and Silas, 'What must I do to be saved?' The implication is that if we work hard enough at it, we can reach the goal. But the misunderstanding here is the failure to see that blackness or salvation (the two are synonymous) is the work of God, not a human work. It is not something we accomplish; it is a gift. That is why Paul and Silas said, 'Believe in the Lord Jesus and you will be saved.'
>
> To *believe* is to receive the gift and utterly to reorient one's existence on the basis of the gift. [...] To receive God's revelation is to become black with God by joining God in the work of liberation.[8]

Repentance has become a cheap transaction, merely professing a creed to join a social club, rather than a life-changing event. Cone's call to become black is an essential corrective. Salvation means more than the redemption of our soul; it must include dying to our status as privileged, white oppressors, and being born again on the side of the poor.

It may seem radical, even heretical, for Cone to claim that salvation and blackness are the same. But when we remember Cone's definition of ontological blackness, this becomes a profound theological declaration. Because God is black, because Christ's Kingdom is for the poor and marginalized, to be a Christian is to follow Christ into solidarity with the least of these. God does not conform to our power structures. In the kingdoms of this world, the winners oppress the losers, the rich the poor, the white the black; but in God's Kingdom, the first shall be last, the last shall be first. The poor and humble are exalted while the rich and powerful are put to shame. To become black with Christ means repentance, putting to death the old nature. We cannot repent in an exclusively spiritual way. Repentance demands our whole life. The Gospel calls the rich to renounce their wealth, the privileged to deny their elite status, and the white to die to whiteness. All oppression must cease in the name of Jesus.

What does it mean to become black? In more practical terms, it is a conscious change of social status, i.e., changing whose side we are on: oppressor or oppressed. By default, most of us accept the status we are born into—which is not necessarily a bad thing. But it becomes a problem if our privileged situation exists at the high cost of excluding, marginalizing, and oppressing others. Whiteness thrives by oppressing blackness. The two positions are interconnected; the privilege of one is a direct result of the other's oppression. If we achieve our status in society because of oppression, then it is sinful. Thus, whiteness is a sin.

Whiteness, for Cone, is thus more about a position in society than a skin tone; it is a statement of solidarity. Whiteness is allegiance to the powerful and wealthy; blackness is solidarity with the poor and oppressed. The harsh reality is that white people are implicit oppressors by birth. Cone explains, "But if you benefit from the past and present injustices committed against blacks, you are partly and indirectly accountable as an American citizen and as a member of the institutions that perpetuate racism."[9] Whether we actively participate in the racist system of oppression created by white supremacy or not, white people benefit from it and agree to it with silent complicity. I, personally, must reckon with the fact that I help prop up a system of oppression whenever I silently accept whiteness.

Cone asks the critical question: "Where is your identity? Where is your being? Does it lie with the oppressed blacks or with the white oppressors?"[10] We must all ask ourselves these questions. There is no middle ground. We either identify radically with Jesus Christ, who is among the least of these, or oppressors. You do not have to be responsible for oppression personally to be complicit in it. Some of the areas where you should examine your privilege include race, class, gender, and sexuality. Privilege may also involve being able-bodied, born in the first world with its wealth and safety, educated, cis-gendered, debt-free, or of sound mind and psychologically healthy. It is worth examining yourself critically and honestly to reckon with your privileges because that is the first step in fighting injustice. Before we repent, we must know the depth of our sinfulness.

Cone explains, "Blackness, then, stands for all victims of oppression who realize that the survival of their humanity is bound up with liberation from whiteness."[11] To be a Christian today in a white-supremacist world is to become black and renounce every privileged status if it means the oppression of others. To become black means to take up solidarity with the oppressed, forgo our privileged status, and join the underprivileged in their struggle for justice. We will never be free until all are free from the oppression of white supremacy.

Solidarity vs. charity

There is a massive difference between charity and solidarity. Philanthropy fails because it merely puts a bandaid over a festering wound. Ultimately, charity props up an oppressive status quo by failing to confront the underlying systemic issues; in fact, it often hides those issues and thus makes matters worse for the oppressed.[12] Charity is when a billionaire gives money to the poor while, at the same time, exploiting their labor for profit. Capitalism only works if there are losers and winners. For the winners to then turn around and arbitrarily help *some* of the losers, while being mostly responsible for their despair, is the height of hypocrisy. The same is true for white people who benefit from white supremacy yet try to fix the problem by offering cheap charitable gestures. Thus, charity is not the ultimate goal. It is a temporary, token act of the privileged few and does not produce lasting systemic change. Charity upholds the status quo rather than disrupting it. It is not a long term strategy. What is required is a complete restructuring of society, not a bandaid.

Charity has, however, been the default mode of Christians in the struggle for justice. But we must be more strategic in fulfilling the mission of Christ to usher in God's Kingdom on Earth as it is in heaven. We must aim for more than short-term solutions; we must strive to disrupt and overthrow the larger systemic structures which keep the poor bound to their poverty and the oppressed stuck in their familiar cycles of oppression.

A defining mark of liberation theology is that it makes sociology its central conversation partner, whereas European theologians often dialogue with philosophy. That is why liberation theology, Cone included, leans heavily on social analysis, particularly Marxism (more on this in the next chapter). Whatever we may conclude about Marx, there is no denying that few have sought to more thoroughly analyze the systems that keep oppressed people bound to oppression.

This affinity with Marx's class analysis is not absolute, but it does highlight the core difference between liberation theology and European theology. While white theology may be content with charity, liberation theology aims to disrupt the systems that cause oppression. In other words, liberation theology asks, "Why are the poor in poverty? Who benefits from oppression? Who benefits from racism?" We must ask questions such as these if we are serious about God's justice. As Cone reminds us, "Christians are called not only to pray for justice but to become actively involved in establishing it. [...] To pray for justice without analyzing the causes of injustice is to turn religion into an opium of the people."[13] Without social analysis, the fight for justice is blind.

It is good to help the poor. Do not misunderstand me. But charity alone is *incomplete* without also striving for systemic change; it is like a doctor easing the symptoms of a disease without trying to cure the disease itself. We must do both. The difference is summarized well by Dom Helder Camara, "When I give food to the poor, they call me a saint. When I ask why the poor have no food, they call me a communist."[14] Donating food and money to the poor may ease our guilty conscience, but it does little to change the system that keeps the poor hungry and penniless. Our compassion for the poor must goad us into asking hard questions about the society we live in, such as *why* the poor starve when there is enough food for everyone or *why* the homeless sleep on our streets when millions of houses sit empty. Why is America the "richest" country in the world but cannot provide healthcare for its citizens as a fundamental human right or pay everyday people a living wage? Yet we can frivolously afford endless wars and a limitless supply of bombs? The truth is, there are more than enough resources to meet everyone's needs, but because we consciously choose to exclude vulnerable people from the table, we enforce a system of sinful oppression.

In racial terms, it is good to give black people positions of leadership and power in society. But we must go beyond token gestures and analyze why they have been excluded from positions of power in the first place. We must ask what systemic policies disproportionately cause more black people to be killed by police or to be criminalized for minor offenses more than white people guilty of the same crimes. We must ask why black families make less money than white families on average. Then we must fight to disrupt the systems that make racism the norm. We must hope and fight for a world where charity is no longer necessary, a world of justice.

There is no neutrality in the struggle for liberation. We are either on the side of the oppressors or the oppressed. We must not be satisfied with becoming *nicer* oppressors by offering occasional charity. Instead, we must forgo our privileged status in society, recognize that we have been complicit in ongoing oppression, and take a radical stand with the oppressed. As Boff warns, "[W]e can be followers of Jesus and true Christians only by making common cause with the poor and working out the gospel of liberation."[15]

Reverse racism?

Is black theology a form of "reverse racism?" Do Black Power and black liberation mean black supremacy, the oppression of whites? Frankly, this sort of argument is socially tone-deaf and ignorant of the black experience, but it is still worth addressing because of how often these concerns arise. As Cone stresses, "Black racism is a myth created by whites to ease their guilt feelings."[16] Black racism is a myth and will remain a myth as long as white supremacy is the norm, until its legacy is rectified.

Carmichael and Hamilton helpfully explain the difference between white power and Black Power, why the former is racist and not the latter:

> There is no analogy—by any stretch of definition or imagination— between the advocates of Black Power and white racists. Racism is not merely exclusion on the basis of race but exclusion for the purpose of subjugating or maintaining subjugation. The goal of racists is to keep black people on the bottom, arbitrarily and dictatorially, as they have done in this country for over three hundred years. The goal of black self-determination and black self-identity—Black Power—is full participation in the decision-making processes affecting the lives of black people. The black people of this country have not lynched whites, bombed their churches, murdered their children and manipulated laws and institutions to maintain oppression. White racists have.[17]

Racism is not personal insults, judgments, or hurt feelings, though this is often what white people assume. Because a black person called them names or harmed their ego, they consider it the epitome of racism.

Whenever a white person feels their privilege is challenged, they cry out reverse racism. "Seeing color" and analyzing the nature of race in society is also considered racism by their fragile white egos. But these definitions miss the point entirely. Racism is any systemic policy or law that marginalizes, oppresses, and targets minority people groups negatively. White people have *never* been the subject of a racist policy in America, but racist policies have almost always targeted people of color.

It comes down to who holds power. As Patricia Bidol explained, racism is "prejudice plus institutional power."[18] Historically, but also up to this present moment, the power is in the hands of white supremacy. Until that changes, black hatred against whites is anger—arguably justified anger—but it is still a far cry from the systemic racism imposed on black people daily.

Calling white supremacy evil is not reverse racism; it is social analysis. White people built America on the backs of African slavery, oppressing black people with lynching and segregation, and today with police brutality and systemic judicial discrimination. White people love to spout the founding myth of American exceptionalism, that they worked for their status in society and earned it. But any success white people have found in America is because of our history of exploiting and brutalizing black men and women. To ignore this is to ignore our past. Racism is the most American thing about America. Our country was built on racist ideals, and it has not changed overnight. Just because black people are no longer enslaved physically, no longer lynched as explicitly, it does not mean they are not enslaved by poverty in the ghettos and lynched by the police. Racism has been modernized, but it has not gone anywhere.

James Cone's theology strives for justice. It is because white people have defined their "rights" by the exploitation and oppression of black people that they feel threatened by the calls for black liberation. By ignoring the history of white brutality, white theology is racist by its silence. White people have been so used to the way things are, to white supremacy, that they nonsensically deem reverse racism anything that even remotely challenges their status in the world. But I hope this book has begun to show why Cone's critique of white Christianity is justified. At the end of this book, I will offer a long reading list for white people questioning the prevalence of white supremacy. We must educate ourselves on the black experience, and until we have humbly listened to their struggle, we have no place to tell black people in America that white supremacy does not affect them.

Being born white is not the issue, but it becomes an issue when a white person uncritically accepts white supremacy as the natural order. It is not having white skin in itself, in the literal sense, that Cone calls sin; instead, it is the ideological adoption of white supremacy that we must condemn as unchristian. The problem is ontological, not physiological, whiteness. Just because we are born into a system of oppression as oppressors does not mean we must align ourselves with that system and assimilate to white supremacy. Instead, Cone's point is that white Christians are called by God to renounce the white supremacist culture in which they live, rather than merely accepting it silently. Christ calls the Church to be counter-cultural, as Cone reminds us, "If the Church is to remain faithful to its Lord, it must make a decisive break with the structure of this society by launching a vehement attack on the evils of racism in all forms."[19]

Whiteness as sin

Cone continues his radical re-interpretation of the Gospel when he declares that "sin is whiteness—the desire of whites to play God in the realm of human affairs."[20] Here whiteness and blackness are not symbols merely of oppressor and the oppressed but of sin and righteousness. White supremacy is sinful; whiteness is a sin because of its allegiance to such an oppressive system. That explains why Cone can make such harsh condemnations of white theology and the white Church. But it also highlights the way liberation theology broadens sin to include more than just personal failure. Sin is social and systemic.

Modern evangelical theology has focused so exclusively on sin as an individual offense against God that it has missed the social and political aspects exemplified by the Bible. Sin is cancer on society. It is not defined by Scripture as a purely moral or spiritual act of *personal* wrongdoing. Instead, the Bible frequently talks about sin in the context of national sins or those of a community.

In the nineteenth century, Schleiermacher was among the first to establish the dogmatic groundwork for a robust social doctrine of sin. He argued that "sinfulness is of a thoroughly collective nature,"[21] and "sin is to be conceived correctly only as the collective act of the human species."[22] It is not the individual alone that sins, since no individual can rightly be understood apart from their community. So while sin is personal, it is not *only* personal, and to ignore the communal dimension of sin is a mistake. The dialectic between a person who sins and the sin of their community is vital. One cannot exist without the other.

Cone argues that whiteness is a sin. That does not mean being white is a sin, but it *is* sinful to affirm white supremacy. Far too often, these are the same, as white people willfully blind themselves from their complicity in ongoing injustice. Just as original sin means no one is free from blame, so being born into a privileged position in society means no one can escape the sins of their community. To ignore white guilt does not make it go away. It is in the best interest of sinners to admit their sin. Likewise, it is in the best interest of white people to acknowledge and repent of their complicity in white supremacy.

Consider the legacy of slavery. America did not earn its wealth. It plundered the labor of African slaves and built its empire on their sweat and blood. While no white person alive today actively participated in slavery, we daily benefit from the legacy of slavery and thus are not blameless. White people are more likely to inherit wealth, property, and social privilege from their parents because of white supremacy. We must realize that being born physically white means inheriting the legacy of colonialism, racism, and oppression; it means benefiting from past injustices.

White moderates may claim innocence, but to be white is to benefit from white supremacy. The only difference is whether we accept that privilege uncritically as the norm or become black with Christ and join the fight to dismantle oppression and liberate the captives. We must be made black with Christ and take up solidarity with the poor and vulnerable in society. We must renounce whiteness in Christ's name.

Social privilege is an expression of original sin. The Christian tradition has long held the belief that we inherit sin at birth, and thus it should not be so difficult for us to see whiteness as inherited sin. Those who take issue with the terms "white supremacy" and "white privilege," yet who accept the doctrine of original sin uncritically, fail to recognize that these express the same problem functionally if not actually.

The Gospel to white America today proclaims liberation from the sin of whiteness, to repent and become black with Christ. White supremacy was put to death in the death of Jesus Christ, and we must renounce our allegiance. Cone's atonement model is unique and highly original in this sense. He highlights the social and political dimensions of sin and links Christ's death with the death of whiteness and white supremacy. It is a kind of political re-interpretation of the Christus Victor model. Just as death is robbed of its power by Christ's death, so whiteness is put to death by Christ suffering under the political humiliation of the powers that be. The Gospel proclaims hope for a new creation without oppressors. To enter into that Kingdom, we must renounce white privilege, repent of whiteness, and be made black with Christ. In other words, we must die to sin and be made new. No longer bound to the oppressive system of racism, the Kingdom of God means freedom for both the oppressor and the oppressed, but it comes at the cost of the oppressors giving up their power. It involves the death of whiteness and the call to be born again together with the black Christ.

To be free is to be black

Dorothee Soelle once profoundly wrote, "The only choice we have is between the absurd cross of meaninglessness and the cross of Christ, the death we accept apathetically as a natural end or the death we suffer as a passion."[23] Suffering is unavoidable. We cannot choose not to suffer. Instead, we must choose between the inevitable suffering of apathy or the suffering and passionate death of Christ's cross. That is, between numbing ourselves in the attempt to avoid pain or leaning into Christ's passion and living life fully alive. Both choices end in death, but the former involves the death of hope before the death of the body, and the latter holds onto the hope of Christ's resurrection by living passionately. "Do not go gentle into that good night" should be the motto of every Christian. We either embrace the cross of Christ or suffer the slow death of paralysis.

The point is this: we are no less free than when we try to be comfortable and safe. The only safety is in the radical passion of the fullness of life. Pain is unavoidable, but we can choose what pain we embrace. We will die standing for what we believe in or die numb and alone on our knees, having sold our souls for comfort and safety. The Kingdom is not safe, but it is worth it. That is the message of Christ's cross.

Black liberation theology is a radical challenge to the white, liberal illusion of false security. To become black with Christ and take up revolutionary solidarity with the poor and oppressed is the only true expression of freedom. Apathy is imprisonment to the idol of cheap comforts.

Repentance from sin is not arbitrary; it is for our good. The Gospel bids us come and die, not because it calls us to a life of unfreedom and sorrow. Instead, Christ calls us to discipleship because this is the best life, life to the fullest. But it is not a life of comfort or safety. We cannot have both comfort and justice. But if we embrace comfort at the expense of true liberty, we will still die and suffer.

To be free is to be black, as Cone writes:

> It is important to point out that freedom is not white middle-class individualism. [...] To be free is to participate with those who are victims of oppression. [...] To be free is to be black—that is, identified with the victims of humiliation in human society and a participate in the liberation of oppressed humanity. The free person in America is the one who does not tolerate whiteness but fights against it, knowing that it is the source of human misery.[24]

Because the oppressor is unfree, dehumanized by their will to power, the only free person is the one who takes up the cause of the oppressed. The false comforts of white middle-class life are illusionary freedoms. No one is truly free until we are all free, until justice reigns and mercy flows. White people will never be free until they take up their neighbors' plight, reject their status as oppressors, and become one with the least of these. True freedom requires justice.

Cone's call to repent and become black with Christ is radical, but so is the Gospel. It is revolutionary because it threatens to kill our comfortable life for a life of struggling for justice. The good life is not the life filled with designer clothes, big houses, and nice things; it is the life lived in God's will, radically joining Christ in solidarity with the least of these, fighting to establish justice on this Earth. It is the life of the Kingdom of God. For the Christian, it is the only true life. May we follow Christ, not our culture of comfort. May we follow Him into radical solidarity with the least of these, become black with Christ, and suffer Christ's cross. We will suffer no matter what. But we can suffer with Christ, which is the only kind of suffering that redeems.

5

THE ETHICS OF LIBERATION

Summary: Black theology is bound to the perspective of an oppressed community, the black Church. The ethics of liberation are under no obligation to submit to the ethics of white oppressors. The distinction is evident in how each ethical perspective responds to the issues of violence, economic inequality, and gender inequality. No one is free until all are free from the tyranny of capitalism, sexism, and racism; the ethics of liberation demand revolutionary praxis—a better world is possible.

In Cone's words:

> Black theology is not academic theology; it is not theology of the dominant classes and racial majorities. It is a theology of the black poor, reconstructing their hopes and dreams of God's coming liberated world.[1]

> Action and thought are related. To know the truth is to do the truth, that is, to make happen in history what is confessed in the church.[2]

> We cannot continue to speak against racism without any reference to a radical change in the economic order. I do not think that racism can be eliminated as long as capitalism remains intact. It is now time for us to investigate socialism as an alternative to capitalism.[3]

Secondary quotes:

> I often became impatient when Christian believers asked me, 'Are you a Marxist?' The best reply that came to mind was this counter-question: 'Do you brush your teeth? I mean, now that the toothbrush has been invented?' How could you read Amos and Isaiah and not Karl Marx and Friedrich Engels? That would amount to being ungrateful to a God who sends prophets among us with the message that to know Yahweh means to do justice. [...] What guided me in this work was recognition that our economic system works for the world's richest people but excludes the vast majority of the human family. [...] [T]he need for analysis arose from the biblical faith in a God of justice.[4]

> — DOROTHEE SOELLE

Introduction

We cannot know God apart from God's liberating act in history, and that means thinking from within the community of the oppressed, where God is present and acts for their liberation. For Cone, black theology is written by and for the black Church. In this sense, black theology did not originate with Cone, as he notes, "Black theology is not something I invented; rather it derives from nearly four hundred years of black struggle for dignity and justice."[5] The importance of the black Church for Cone cannot be overstated.

In this chapter, we will consider the ethics of the black community. Because the perspective of the oppressed determines the ethics of liberation, it is necessarily at odds with the judgments of their oppressors. That is what sets Cone's ethical reflections apart from white theological ethics, resulting in a unique response to violence, capitalism, and sexism. Here the perspective of the oppressed becomes more clearly at odds with that of the oppressor, and thus it reveals the underlying contradiction between white and black theology: *Who does theology speak for?*

A focus on oppressed communities leads, necessarily, to intersectionality. The liberation of one must include the liberation of all oppressed people. Race, class, and gender are all interconnected. Thus, Cone challenges the black Church, and theology as a whole, to take Marxism and black feminism more seriously as viable conversation partners. We must fight to overcome the idolatry of Mammon, which means taking Marx's critique of capital seriously. The Church should adopt a socialist stance in the fight against injustice. The contribution of Marxism is far too important for the Church to allow the propaganda of Western capitalists to drown out its voice. As the community of the oppressed, the Church is an ally of anyone who takes the plight of the poor seriously. Likewise, we must be allies of black feminism, denouncing our historical complicity in the patriarchy.

Violence

One of the central issues in the ethics of liberation is the question of violence. But the question is not between violence and non-violence, as often supposed. By soberly assessing the material conditions of oppressed communities, we have to recognize that the violence suffered in these communities far outweighs any violence enacted in protest. Structural violence affects the black community more severely than any riot that erupts in response. Oppression *violently* robs the oppressed of their right to essential human dignities such as clean water, suitable housing, health care, a living wage, and high-quality education. So the question of violence does matter, but not in the way we often think. The more important question we must ask is this: *Whose* violence are we more concerned with? The violence of an oppressive status quo, or the revolt of the oppressed against their oppressor?

Cone is far more concerned with the violence of structural oppression. He writes, "[T]he problem of violence is not the problem of a few black revolutionaries but the problem of a whole social structure which outwardly appears to be ordered and respectable but inwardly is 'ridden by psychopathic obsessions and delusions'—racism and hatred."[6] The white moderate calling for "law and order" aims to uphold the status quo, but they fail to see how the established order marginalizes and condemns the poor and black to live in subhuman conditions because of racist policies. White support for the status quo, even silent support, is in itself a form of violence. In a violent, unjust, racist society, neutrality is impossible. Non-violence is an illusion of the privileged. As Cone writes, "Violence is embedded in American law, and it is blessed by the keepers of moral sanctity."[7] Thus, "It is important to point out that no one can be nonviolent in an unjust society."[8]

The white liberals who decry protestors rioting and looting while remaining silent about the ongoing violence of systemic oppression are not genuinely concerned with violence. The violent systems that create ghettos, permit police brutality, rip families apart through mass incarceration, and confine millions to poverty do not concern them because it does not affect them. The violent oppression of black and poor people establishes their comfortable middle-class lifestyle; it is the foundation of their privilege. Riots disrupt their comfortable privilege with a hard dose of reality, the reality of the underclass. Martin Luther King, Jr., explained, "A riot is the language of the unheard." The oppressed are not at peace, they are denied justice, and that is why they riot. The marginalized have no voice or stake in society, which is why they loot and steal in protest against the system that oppresses them (as seen in the global antiracist demonstrations following the lynching of George Floyd in 2020).

We either side with the violence of the oppressors or with their victims. White moderates often define their ethics according to state laws, but in an unjust society, legality itself can be unethical. It is legal for a white cop to kill a black teenager for nothing and with no repercussions. It is legal for society to rob the poor's future by denying them access to basic human rights. Slavery and lynching were also legal, and white moderates were quick to call it ethical accordingly. But Cone argues that the oppressor has no moral standing to determine what is or is not ethical for the people they oppress. The ethics of liberation do not have to answer the concerns of the oppressor.

American history is ugly, racist, and inhumane, but we will never heal until we recognize and repent of our past. As Faulkner wrote, "The past is never dead. It's not even past."[9] The worst path forward is to ignore our history or try to whitewash it with a nationalistic myth. The bloody history of colonialism, slavery, genocide, imperialism, and segregation is still present in America today; it is the foundation of our society. This legacy is alive and well in America's systemic violence against black and poor people, the economic ghettoization of black neighborhoods and schools, the systemic imprisonment of black men and women, police violence with impunity, and societal and political exclusion. Outside America's borders, in the imperialistic exploitation of black bodies in the third world, we are no better off. We have only become better at hiding our atrocities under the banner of freedom and security. Consider how, in the name of "fighting terrorism," America has enacted far greater terrors with its perpetuation of endless war.

America is guilty of killing approximately 245,000 *civilians*—innocent men, women, and children—in the war on terror. That's about one hundred times the death toll of 9/11 (2,757). For every American who died in that tragedy, we have murdered one hundred civilians abroad. But because they are black Arabs from the Middle East and not white Americans, their deaths are merely a speedbump to American exceptionalism. Violent white oppressors have no right to turn to the poor and black oppressed people of the world and condemn their violence; that is tantamount to ignoring Christ's warning, "Why do you see the speck in your neighbor's eye, but do not notice the log in your own eye?" (Matthew 7:5).

Cone explains:

> It is this fact that most whites seem to overlook—the fact that violence already exists. The Christian does not decide between violence and nonviolence, evil and good. He decides between the less and the greater evil. He must ponder whether revolutionary violence is less or more deplorable than the violence perpetrated by the system.[10]

Thus, it is up to the oppressed to determine the means of their liberation. The oppressor has no right to condemn the violence of the oppressed. Nor can the oppressed afford to wait for their oppressor to devise a means of liberation for them. Black liberation cannot wait for white moderates to "get around to it." The oppressed must decide for themselves the actions they will take to overthrow their oppressors. If that includes violence, then so be it. No one gives up power without a struggle. If white supremacy is to be dismantled and overcome, it is unlikely it will go without a fight. We hope and pray that justice comes peacefully. But when the established order is vicious and violent, killing and brutalizing millions of the poor and black, then the revolutionary activities of the underclass will always be the lesser evil in the struggle for justice.[11]

Liberation demands revolution

Reform is not enough. The ethics of liberation demand revolution. In a structurally violent society, the only ethical option is to dismantle the systems of bondage and overthrow its structures of oppression. Liberation does not aim to *improve* this world; it demands a better world altogether. Another world is possible and necessary. The hope for such a world drives revolution. This hope also inspires the Christian faith. We hope for the

Kingdom of God. If we are idealistic, if we demand "too much," it is for Christ's sake.

Ethics do not belong in the classroom. Abstract thought experiments help no one. Not to act, not to fight for justice, is to deny the mission of Christ; it is to deny our resurrection hope for a world without oppression. To be ethical in an unethical world means refusing to stay silent wherever injustice prevails. The ethics of liberation are an ethic of revolution. There can be no peace until oppression ceases, and justice reigns. All power to the people.

The ethics of liberation demand revolutionary action because the struggle is *God's* struggle. Our God is the God of justice and thus of revolution. Only by joining in God's liberating act *within* the oppressed community can we begin to ask about ethics, which excludes white, rich oppressors from pronouncing judgments about how those they oppress are fighting back against their oppression. The man of power with a proverbial boot on the neck of the oppressed is in no position to teach ethics.

The goal of liberation is a world free from oppression. Does this mean retaliation? Cone argues no; vengeance is never the goal because it merely makes the oppressed into oppressors, thus perpetuating the cycle. Cone writes:

> Our intention is not to make the oppressors the slaves but to transform humanity, or, in the words of Fanon, 'set afoot a new man.' Thus hatred and vengeance have no place in the struggle for freedom. [...] The ethic of liberation arises out of love, for ourselves and for humanity. This is an essential ingredient of liberation without which the struggle turns into a denial of what divine liberation means.[12]

The goal of liberation culminates in King's vision of a "Beloved Community" in which enemies become friends through love. But until the social order changes, that dream remains just a dream; the oppressors must be free from their will to power, and the oppressed must find new footing from under the weight of bondage. God is on the side of the oppressed *because* God is moving human history towards this beloved community, which we would accurately call the Kingdom of God. It is an eschatological concept that cannot remain inaccessible to us in some far off dream. The goal of liberation is, "Thy Kingdom come, thy will be done, on Earth as it is in heaven!"

Liberation is the priority. But many today, especially in the white Church, call for "reconciliation," as if it were possible *before* liberation. The white Church uses this in the context of black people reconciling themselves with white people as if *they* are the ones with the problem! As if they have been the oppressors! But reconciliation without liberation means forcing the oppressed to acclimate themselves to their oppression. It is unjust. Reconciliation without justice defines victims by their victimization. As Cone explains:

> To be reconciled with white people means destroying their oppressive power, reducing them to the human level and thereby putting them on equal footing with other humans. There can be no reconciliation with masters, as long as men are in prison. There can be no communication between masters and slaves until masters no longer exist, are no longer present as masters.[13]

The oppressor has no moral right to call for reconciliation and forgiveness when they are responsible for the violence done to the oppressed. White Christians are quick to talk about reconciliation with black people because it allows them to pretend that the problem is not with them. Yes, black people may be angry, but who are we to say they need to learn how to forget the past and forgive white people? What hypocrisy! That is like stabbing a man, then commanding him to forgive and be reconciled to you while the knife is still in his back. Until the black community is *genuinely* free from systemic racism, there will never be reconciliation. Reconciliation is impossible until liberation is the reality of all people. White moderates calling for reconciliation without justice are violent and hypocritical. We must, as a Church, give up this kind of language. We must adopt the attitude of total liberation and revolutionary change.

Marxism

What defines the Church? What makes it *Christ's* Church and not another's? The Church is not primarily determined according to its creeds, traditions, or even its theology, as we often think. Instead, as Cone argues, the Church of Jesus Christ is primarily defined by its commitment to the poor:

> The church is that people who have been called into being by the life,

death, and resurrection of Jesus so that they can bear witness to Jesus' Lordship by participating with him in the struggle of freedom. This means that the primary definition of the church is not its confessional affirmations but rather its political commitment on behalf of the poor.[14]

We are Christ's Church if we follow Christ's way. Yet we often focus more on creedal fidelity than the ethical and political imperatives of the Gospel. But to genuinely be the Church of Christ, we must follow Him into solidarity with the least of these, the poor, weak, and black.

It is one thing to be concerned about the well-being of the poor, but it is another to ask: Why are they poor? Who benefits from their poverty? Why is it that in the wealthiest country on the face of the Earth, 40 million Americans live in poverty? Why is there such a stark disparity between the rich and poor? And why do forty percent of middle-class, working Americans live on the brink of poverty, into which they will sink if they miss even a single paycheck?[15]

These questions highlight why social analysis is necessary for accomplishing the Church's mission. Cone writes, "Real substantial change in societal structures requires scientific analysis."[16] It is not enough to put a band-aid over the wound and pretend that we have fixed the underlying issues. We must fight for a system where all people can live and flourish, a society that does not think it is "normal" for anyone to die from unmet needs while others hoard more wealth than they could spend in a thousand lifetimes. There are enough resources to go around; there is enough food and water and shelter for everyone. But why do so many people in this rich country go hungry, lack clean water, and live on the streets? Capitalism is a system designed to exploit the many for the profit of the few. When millions starve or perish from malnourishment, *capitalism is working as designed.* It is a system that cannot survive unless there are winners and losers. But it is an unchristian system, and a better world is possible.

It is not enough for us to temporarily fix the symptoms of injustice (poverty); the Church must focus its efforts on confronting the disease itself (capitalism). We must fight the underlying causes that keep people homeless, hungry, and dehumanized by the harsh realities of poverty. But if we do not know what causes injustice, we cannot fight against it. That is where Marxism is a useful sociological tool. Marx's critique of capital is not perfect, but it helps us imagine a world beyond poverty and economic disparity. As Denys Munby astutely realized: "If modern marxism gives the wrong answers, at least it asks the right questions."[17]

No one should die from a lack of money, yet this happens daily under capitalism as the vital essentials for life are privatized for the profit of a few privileged individuals. As Cone writes, "The earth is the Lord's and its resources are intended for all. No one has a right to control by private ownership the necessities of human life."[18] In an unplanned economy, the rich will always exploit the poor. Socialism offers a viable alternative by strategically prioritizing human life over capital gains.

A standard critique of liberation theology is that its use of Marx is theologically untenable. By merely learning from Marxism, it is rejected as a false Gospel. This attack often relies more on Western propaganda against socialism than on any real insight into what it expounds. Rejecting an idea before understanding it is engaging in bad faith politics, especially when that idea threatens the established order. Thus, those in power are more likely to do everything they can to spread misinformation. The result is that Marxism is a dirty word in the Western world, but this is not enough reason for rejecting it outright. We must go beyond these cheap misrepresentations and soberly assess Marx's value; in his efforts to analyze capitalism's inner workings, Marx's insights are too important to ignore.

But it is crucial to recognize that Marxism is never more than a useful *tool* for Cone. It does not replace theology or become an ideological master. Marxism does not replace the Gospel, but rather, as Leonardo and Clodovis Boff explain, "liberation theology uses Marxism purely as an *instrument.*"[19] We should distinguish between Marxism as a *worldview* and Marxism as an *instrument* of social analysis. Liberation theology rejects the former and embraces the latter. We can and should learn from Marxism without it becoming our controlling ideology. Marxism, however helpful, will always come second to the Gospel. Yet it is precisely *because* the Gospel compels us to take up the cause of the poor that we should learn from Marx.

Cone argues, "Marxism can be understood as a scientific tool for analyzing the economic, political, and social structures of this society so that we will know how to actualize in the world the freedom that we affirm in faith."[20] Just as the Church would be foolish to reject the fruit of modern science in the form of life-saving medicine and life-improving technology, we would be foolish to dismiss the critical contribution of the social sciences to how we understand the world. Cone asks, "How can we participate in the liberation of the poor from oppression if we do not know *who* the poor are and *why* they live in poverty?"[21] Marxism helps us understand "why the social, economic, and political orders are arranged as they are. It enables us to know who benefits from the status quo."[22] Fighting for liberation without accepting the help of tools such as Marxism means fighting blindly.

Marxism and the Christian faith can learn from each other and would benefit from sustained dialogue. Both share the hope of a better world, as well as the drive to care for the poor, fight for justice, and overcome the worship of Mammon. Yet most Western Christians unthinkingly reject Marxism, likely because of years of propaganda against socialism in the American media and even in the Church. But ultimately, as Cone argues, "Marxism is too important to be allowed to be buried in its misrepresentations. Christians must undertake to clarify and reinterpret Marxism, so that it can serve as a useful tool for discovering how capitalism functions."[23]

The Church today cannot fear the truth, no matter where it originates. If the truth comes from Karl Marx's class analysis, we would be foolish to ignore it. Like Schleiermacher's concept of the "eternal covenant" between faith and science—in which the truths of faith and the truths of science coincide and mutually benefit each other—so Cone argues for a covenant between faith and sociology. We would benefit from a Christianity more sociologically informed in its political conclusions. If our God is the God of truth, then we should never fear the truth, no matter its origin.

By ignoring sociological insights such as those found in Marxism, we default to our culture's presuppositions. In America, that is the neo-liberal, corporatist, capitalist position, which is guilty of oppressing millions of people around the world for the profit of a few wealthy billionaires.[24] The cultural norms of our society cannot be accepted uncritically. So we must lean into sociological analysis to learn the best position for the Christian to take in social and political issues, particularly any analysis that helps us understand poverty and work to overcome its systemic oppression.

We cannot afford to forget: "People are not poor by accident. They are *made* poor by the rich and powerful few."[25] Poverty is not inevitable. Once we realize that poverty is abnormal, that a better world is possible, we will fight for a world without the tyranny of capital. As Cone continues, "This means that to do liberation theology, one must make a commitment, an option for the poor and against those who are responsible for their poverty."[26] The Church must adopt a socialist position for Christ's sake. A political commitment to the poor is what makes the Church *Christ's* Church. We will not rightly fulfill our calling without critically analyzing the conditions that systemically produce poverty and fight against all forms of oppression.

It may seem unrealistic to hope for a world beyond capitalism. But that is precisely the nature of Christian hope; it is not rooted in what we can see. Cone writes, regarding those who argue that socialism is an impossible hope:

> If we limit our hope to what is, then we destroy it. Hope is the expectation of that which is not. It is a belief that the impossible is possible, the 'not yet' is coming in history. Without hope, the people perish. [...] To believe in God is to know that our hope is grounded in Jesus Christ, the crucified Lord whose resurrected presence creates a new hope for a better world. Why not think that the 'not yet' is possible? Why not think of a completely new society and begin to devise ways to realize it on earth?[27]

May our hope be larger than our doubt, and may we fight for a better tomorrow in the name of Jesus Christ. By whatever means necessary, we must fight to overthrow all systems of oppression, including the tyranny of capital. The poor are Christ's people. As Boff writes, "The rights of the poor are God's rights."[28] But our concern for the poor must go beyond cheap charity. We must fight to overthrow the chains that keep the poor in bondage and liberate all people from the idolatry of Mammon. We must strive with the poor for a better world in the name of Jesus Christ and His coming Kingdom.

Black feminism

Black women are one of the most oppressed groups in history. One of Cone's regrets about his early work was its lack of attention to the plight of black women suffering under the dual weight of racism and sexism. He writes, "The most glaring limitation of *A Black Theology of Liberation* was my failure to be receptive to the problem of sexism in the black community and society as a whole."[29]

The issues of race, class, and sex are deeply intertwined; true liberation requires the destruction of all systems of injustice. Liberation must be intersectional. Thus, the success of liberation is bound to the success of black feminism. As Cone challenged the black Church to adopt an anti-capitalist stance, so he urges a radical commitment to overthrow the patriarchal systems that keep women in bondage. The Church must learn from the suffering of black women and repent of its complicity in their oppression.

Theressa Hoover writes, "To be a woman, black, and active in religious institutions in the American scene is to labor under triple jeopardy."[30] I want to briefly examine some of the ways black women have experienced double, triple, even quadruple jeopardy in America. The experience of oppressed black women in our midst is Christ's Word to the Church today, the revelation of God's solidarity with the oppressed.

Black women are the fastest-growing prison population in America, and 60% of those behind bars are mothers with children under 18.[31] In addition to the emotional, physical, and psychological trauma common to men's prisons, incarcerated women are often sexually abused with relative impunity. Corrections officers use strip searches and invasive body cavity searches to abuse and humiliate women. They regularly monitor showers and bathrooms, further denying women the right to personal dignity. According to a recent report, female inmates in New Jersey were forced by guards to exchange sex for essentials like toilet paper.[32] These abuses are seldom reported—If a guard abuses you, who will you tell? Another guard?—but for those that are reported, the perpetrators are rarely punished. The savage legacy of slaveholders raping and abusing vulnerable black women persists today in the mass incarceration of women and the sexual abuses that follow. America uses its prisons to store unwanted and marginalized people, which creates a culture of normalizing violence against prisoners because they are "bad" people who deserve their imprisonment. But no human being deserves to suffer these cruel injustices. It is a horrendous evil often ignored in discussions of liberation and social justice. Prisons are harsh and dangerous for men, but they can be twice as brutal for women.[33]

Impoverished black women are also more likely to be evicted from their homes and thrown out on the streets.[34] One of the reasons for the disparity is the gender wage-gap. Women are more likely to work in lower-paying jobs, while men with the same education and skills are more likely to find higher-paying employment in the same neighborhoods. It is impossible to support a family and pay rent with the current minimum wage in America, which is far below a living wage. Children also contribute to the disparity, since landlords are under close legal scrutiny whenever children are present. Accordingly, landlords are more likely to rent their properties to childless families or individuals. Even the possibility of future pregnancy can hinder the availability of housing for black women. These factors lead to a widespread marginalization and oppression of black women and black single mothers seeking affordable housing.

Black women have the highest maternal fatality rate in America, more than double that of white women.[35] Although both groups should, in theory, receive the same quality of medical care, there is an apparent disparity in the care shown to black women in maternity wards. The lack of adequate health care for black women, including the biases they face whenever care is available, is a massive problem we must resolve. Free universal health care for all will be an essential first step in overcoming this injustice. Because black women are more likely to experience poverty, they are also less likely to afford quality health insurance. This is where the triple jeopardy comes in: poor black women are positioned to receive the shortest end of the stick, the worst deal for medical care because of institutional racism, classism, and sexism.

Mainstream feminists tend to marginalize the perspective of black feminists. White feminists—supposedly allies in a shared struggle—often overlook black feminists' racial concerns, marginalize their stories, or silence their voices altogether. The message white-feminists subtly affirm by their actions is that feminism is a white woman's issue. White feminists often prioritize their whiteness *over* and thus *against* black women and their struggles. They are more ideologically committed to white supremacy than the liberation of *all* women, especially women of color. Like a wolf in sheep's clothing, white feminists often play the activist card when it suits their interests, but consistently marginalize black women whenever it threatens their privilege.

In the Church, black women are no less marginalized. Women in the Church suffer from a long history of male dominance, which is often justified by literalist, sexist interpretations of the Bible, not unlike how white Christians justified slavery. Women's voices are often silenced or suppressed by their male counterparts. Women are refused the dignity of leadership, except the leadership over other women. Even when women are more qualified for the task, men are more likely to fill leadership positions. It is an injustice cloaked in the name of old-world, "biblical" values. The message most Churches preach from the pulpit supports patriarchal oppression in the family and community rather than challenging its sexist assumptions. The Church's allegiance to sexism runs deep, and its effect is felt in the ways we have been complicit in male brutality against women. The Church must see itself through the eyes of the women it has oppressed for so long on account of its allegiance to an outdated ideology of male dominance. We should be at the forefront of the fight against oppression, yet we are far too often defenders of the status quo.

These brief considerations only skim the surface of the many challenges black women face as they live at the intersection of two or three oppressed identities: black, female, and often poor. If we are indeed a Church that cares for the least of these, then our fight for liberation must be intersectional. We must listen to the underprivileged, especially those who suffer under multiple forms of oppression. We should also expand intersectionality to include the plight of LGBTQ+ individuals and all those who have been marginalized because of their sexual orientation or non-conforming gender identity. A poor, black, transgender woman faces quadruple jeopardy by living at the intersection of four oppressed identities, and therefore, the likelihood of abuse, violence, and discrimination increases fourfold. The Gospel must be intersectional. As Christ's Church, we must be concerned with the plight of oppressed people everywhere.

CONCLUSION

"The prophet is a man who feels fiercely."[1] So writes Abraham J. Heschel in his classic book on the subject. A prophet is not a passive mouthpiece for God; he or she is a person inflamed with God's *pathos*, a partner in the passionate concerns of heaven. The prophet affirms with their whole being God's involvement in human affairs. God is not impersonal or indifferent; God is concerned for us. As Heschel explains, "The foundational experience of the prophet is a fellowship with the feelings of God, a *sympathy with the divine pathos*."[2] God's passionate concern for the human race is the prophet's burden. Heschel further writes:

> God has thrust a burden upon his soul, and he is bowed and stunned at man's fierce greed. Frightful is the agony of man; no human voice can convey its full terror. Prophecy is the voice that God has lent to the silent agony, a voice to the plundered poor, to the profaned riches of the world. It is a form of living, a crossing point of God and man. God is raging in the prophet's words.[3]

Accordingly, the prophet is "an iconoclast, challenging the apparently holy, revered, and awesome. Beliefs cherished as certainties, institutions endowed with supreme sanctity, he exposes as scandalous pretensions."[4] No description is more apt for the life and theology of James Cone. He is likely the most exceptional prophetic voice in the American Church. If he appears angry, hostile to the status quo, and disruptive to theological norms, then it is because he has heard the heart of God's passionate concern for the least of these. Indeed, "God is raging in the prophet's words." His iconoclasm is one of prophetic disruption, the refusal to accept things as they are. He strives for the Kingdom of God on this Earth with every passionate rebuke against white supremacy, every outburst against the color-blind heresy of theological racism, and every protest against a complicit white Church.

Cone is a poignant reminder that theology is not just a language game; there are real stakes involved. The God revealed in Christ is deeply concerned with justice. Theology must, too, be concerned with making all things right, which requires conflict with every reality that falls short. Cheap peace only helps the oppressor. We must fight for righteousness in the name of God and the Kingdom that is coming. As Cone writes:

> Creative theological thinking is born out of conflict, the recognition that what *is* is *not* true, even though untruth has established itself as true. Theology has a critical, prophetic task. It should interpret the truth of the gospel for the times in which we live so that it has continuity with the past but also challenges and exposes the present contradictions, thereby empowering the oppressed to make a new future for themselves.[5]

We need theologians like Cone, who continuously disrupt the status quo. The pronouncement that Jesus Christ is Lord means the Church must stand up against racism, sexism, poverty, and injustice in all its forms. "If the Church is to remain faithful to its Lord," Cone writes, "it must make a decisive break with the structure of this society by launching a vehement attack on the evils of racism in all forms. It must become *prophetic,* demanding a radical change in the interlocking structures of this society."[6]

The impact of Cone's theology on my life has been profound. When I was young, a consistent prayer of mine was that God would enlarge my heart to know and feel the concerns of God's heart for the least of these. This book is radical, and perhaps a bit shocking to read. But I believe it is the culmination of that boyhood prayer. The plight of oppressed people around the world is God's concern. May it become ours. God, enlarge our hearts! May we seek justice and righteousness and freedom for the oppressed, poor, weak, and powerless.

I hope and pray that Cone's influence only grows in the Church. I have tried to show the radical truth of his theology with this book because I believe that James Cone is vital for the Church today. I pray his prophetic voice is heard and heeded more and more. May we catch his vision of God's involvement in the history of liberation and join in God's revolutionary struggle. The Church can no longer remain a champion of the status quo. May we become the revolutionary community of the oppressed, fighting in the Divine struggle for liberation. The Gospel is the pronouncement of liberation—that all oppression must cease in the name of the One who raised Christ from the dead. May His Kingdom come and will be done on Earth as it is in heaven. Amen.

FURTHER READING

No book in my "Plain English" series is an end unto itself, and this one is no exception. I always hope to send my readers on a journey to discover for themselves the theologians I discuss. Here we will talk about some of the primary, secondary, and peripheral texts that helped me write this book.

A guide to the books by James Cone

The three central texts for understanding James Cone's theology are *God of the Oppressed, A Black Theology of Liberation,* and *Black Theology and Black Power.* If you read only these texts, you will still gain a firm understanding of what makes Cone's theology significant. They were the most helpful books in my writing.

God of the Oppressed is arguably Cone's most systematic work. *A Black Theology of Liberation* comes second to that text for its systematic rigor. Both make up the core of Cone's theology. And finally, the passion of his first book, *Black Theology and Black Power,* is unsurpassed even if it does not always reflect Cone's mature thought. I cannot recommend these three texts highly enough.

The Cross and the Lynching Tree and *My Soul Looks Back* are the next two most essential books in Cone's corpus. *My Soul Looks Back* offers important biographical reflections, which is vital for understanding Cone.

But *The Cross and the Lynching Tree* is less of a book and more of a life-changing experience. It would be unlikely for anyone to read that book and put it down unchanged by the force of its vision. It is an incredibly profound work, and perhaps a more fitting introduction to Cone's thought than any other text even if it lacks some of the systematic rigor of the first three I mentioned.

The Spirituals and the Blues is an important early work not to be overlooked. It is especially notable as Cone begins to develop black theology solely on the basis of the black experience in America.

Said I Wasn't Gonna Tell Nobody, Cone's final book, was published posthumously. It is a valuable biographical reflection.

Martin & Malcolm & America is an insightful study and particularly helpful for understanding Cone's relation to both figures.

For my People and *Speaking the Truth* are Cone's ecumenical books, written for the black Church specifically but have an important bearing on the Church as a whole.

Risks of Faith compiles some of Cone's best essays, including his first publication on black theology. The two-volume series Cone co-edited with Gayraud S. Wilmore is also insightful: *Black Theology: A Documentary History*.

Although Cone did not publish a tremendous amount of books, what he lacks for in pages he makes up in the strength of his vision and the vigor of his critique. With these books, he dismantled the supremacy of white theology and paved the way for the black perspective in America and beyond.

Several lectures are freely available online. These are especially helpful in discerning the tone and passion behind Cone's thought:

"The Cross & The Lynching Tree." June 1, 2012. https://www.youtube.com/watch?v=-lhPNP3GIyY.

"A Conversation with James Cone." January 6, 2014. https://www.youtube.com/watch?v=a7NKXlmRvWE.

"Strange Fruit: The Cross and the Lynching Tree." Harvard Divinity School, June 2, 2014. https://www.youtube.com/watch?v=ZngcqqgQyzo.

"Fifth Annual Niebuhr Forum on Religion in Public Life." Elmhurst University, March 24, 2015. https://www.youtube.com/watch?v=AWC0ZKSWw_Y.

"2015 MLK Lecture with Professor James H. Cone." Duke Divinity

School, April 7, 2015. https://www.youtube.com/watch?v=ziEGUYKkVGY.

"The Cry of Black Blood: The Rise of Black Liberation Theology." Union Theological Seminary, February 25, 2016. https://www.youtube.com/watch?v=P_Q768HvabU.

"The Cry of Black Blood." Yale Divinity School, April 20, 2017. https://www.youtube.com/watch?v=kyP7BrmII9U&t=814s.

"James Cone's Final Interview." April 7, 2019. https://www.youtube.com/watch?v=kR3-z1xHgPY.

Books about James Cone

The secondary literature on Cone is minimal. Although he is one of the most important theologians of recent history, he has not yet inspired the level of examination I think he deserves. There have been a few books on his work, however, which I list here:

Barger, Lilian Calles. *The World Come of Age: An Intellectual History of Liberation Theology.*

Burrow, Jr., Rufus. *James H. Cone and Black Liberation Theology.*

Hopkins, Dwight N., and Edward P. Antonio, editors. *The Cambridge Companion to Black Theology.*

Hopkins, Dwight N., editor. *Black Faith and Public Talk: Critical Essays on James H. Cone's* Black Theology & Black Power.

Singleton, III, Harry H. *Black Theology and Ideology: Deideological dimensions in the theology of James H. Cone.*

Books for a perpetual antiracist education and understanding of the black experience

Reading James Cone is a great place to start, but it is only the beginning of a lifelong journey to become an ally in the fight for black liberation. It is vital, especially as a white person, to be continually learning from the black experience. In our privilege, it is easy to turn a blind eye to the suffering of the oppressed, but we must not become apathetic. If God reveals Godself in the plight of the least of these, then it is a Christian obligation to listen to the voices of the oppressed. That involves a lifelong commitment to reading and studying the words of the black, poor, and underprivileged. Here I present a list of resources, many of which were vital for me in writing this book—listed alphabetically.

Alexander, Michelle. *The New Jim Crow: Mass Incarceration in the Age of Colorblindness.* 2010.

Baldwin, James. *Go Tell It on the Mountain*
—*If Beale Street Could Talk*
—*James Baldwin: Collected Essays.*
—*Notes of a Native Son*
—*The Fire Next Time.*

Baptist, Edward E. *The Half Has Never Been Told: Slavery and the Making of American Capitalism.*

Baradaran, Mehrsa. *The Color of Money: Black Banks and the Racial Wealth Gap.*

Beauvoir, Simone De. *The Second Sex.*

Berry, Daina Ramey; Kali Nicole Gross. *A Black Women's History of the United States.*

Blackmon, Douglas A. *Slavery by Another Name: The Re-Enslavement of Black Americans from the Civil War to World War II.*

Boesak, Allan. *Black and Reformed: Apartheid, Liberation and the Calvinist Tradition.*

Brown, Austin Channing. *I'm Still Here: Black Dignity in a World Made for Whiteness.*

Carmichael, Stokely; Hamilton, Charles V. *Black Power: The Politics of Liberation.*

Coates, Ta-Nehisi. *Between the World and Me.*

Carter, J. Kameron. *Race: A Theological Account.*

Davis, Angela Y. *An Autobiography.*
—*Are Prisons Obsolete?*
—*Freedom Is a Constant Struggle.*
—*If They Come in the Morning: Voices of Resistance.*
—*Women, Race, and Class.*

Douglas, Kelly Brown. *Black Bodies and Black Church: A Blues Slant.*
—*The Black Christ.*
—*Sexuality in the Black Church: A Womanist Perspective.*
—*Stand Your Ground: Black Bodies and the Justice of God.*

Du Bois, W. E. B. *Black Reconstruction in America*

Dyson, Michael Eric. *Tears We Cannot Stop: A Sermon to White America.*

—*What Truth Sounds Like: Robert F. Kennedy, James Baldwin, and Our Unfinished Conversation About Race in America.*

Eddo-Lodge, Reni. *Why I'm No Longer Talking To White People About Race.*

Ellison, Ralph. *Invisible Man.*

Fanon, Frantz. *Black Skin, White Masks.*

—*The Wretched of the Earth.*

Jennings, Willie. *Christian Imagination: Theology and the Origins of Race.*

Harvey, Paul. *The Color of Christ: The Son of God and the Saga of Race in America.*

Hughes, Langston. *Montage of a Dream Deferred.*

—*Poems.*

James, C. L. R. *The Black Jacobins.*

Kendi, Ibram X. *How to Be an Antiracist.*

—*Stamped from the Beginning: The Definitive History of Racist Ideas in America.*

King Jr., Martin Luther. *Letter from the Birmingham Jail.*

—*Strength to Love.*

—*The Autobiography of Martin Luther King, Jr.*

—*The Radical King* (ed. by Cornell West).

—*Where Do We Go from Here: Chaos or Community?*

—*Why We Can't Wait.*

Levi, Robin; Ayelet Waldman, ed. *Inside This Place, Not of It: Narratives from Women's Prisons.*

Lincoln, C. Eric, editor. *The Black Experience in Religion.*

Morrison, Toni. *Beloved*

—*Song of Solomon*

—*The Bluest Eye*

Oluo, Ijeoma. *So You Want to Talk About Race.*

Rothstein, Richard. *The Color of Law: A Forgotten History of How Our Government Segregated America.*

Saad, Layla. *Me and White Supremacy: Combat Racism, Change the World, and Become a Good Ancestor.*

Schenwar, Maya. *Who Do You Serve, Who Do You Protect? Police Violence and Resistance in the United States.*

Sivanandan, Ambalavaner. *Communities of Resistance: Writings on Black Struggles for Socialism.*

Tatum, Beverly Daniel. *"Why Are All The Black Kids Sitting Together in the Cafeteria?": A Psychologist Explains the Development of Racial Identity.*

Taylor, Keeanga-Yamahtta. *From #BlackLivesMatter to Black Liberation.*

—*How We Get Free: Black Feminism and the Combahee River Collective.*

Thomas, Linda E., editor. *The Living Stones in the Household of God: The Legacy and Future of Black Theology.*

Thurman, Howard. *Jesus and the Disinherited.*

Tisby, Jemar. *The Color of Compromise: The Truth about the American Church's Complicity in Racism.*

Tyson, Timothy B. *The Blood of Emmett Till.*

Wallis, Jim. *America's Original Sin: Racism, White Privilege, and the Bridge to a New America.*

Wells, Ida B. *Crusade for Justice: The Autobiography of Ida B. Wells.*

—*Southern Horrors.*

—*The Light of Truth.*

West, Cornel. *Black Prophetic Fire*

—*Democracy Matters: Winning the Fight Against Imperialism.*

—*Prophesy Deliverance!*

—*Race Matters.*

X, Malcolm. *Malcom Speaks.*

—*The Autobiography of Malcolm X.*

General bibliography

Alves, Rubem A. *A Theology of Human Hope.*

Barth, Karl. *Against the Stream: Shorter Post-War Writings, 1945-52.*

—*Church Dogmatics.*

Bentley, James. *Between Marx and Christ.*

Boff, Leonardo; Boff, Clodovis. *Introducing Liberation Theology.*

Boff, Leonardo. *Cry of the Earth, Cry of the Poor.*

—*Jesus Christ Liberator: A Critical Christology for Our Time.*

Bonhoeffer, Dietrich. *Discipleship* (DBW Vol. 4).

—*Ethics* (DBW Vol. 6).

—*Letters and Papers from Prison* (DBW Vol. 8).

Bregman, Rutger. *Utopia for Realists: How We Can Build the Ideal World.*

Chomsky, Noam. *How the World Works.*

—*On Anarchism.*

—*Profit Over People: Neoliberalism and Global Order.*

—*Who Rules the World?*

Daly, Mary. *Beyond God the Father: Toward a Philosophy of Woman's Liberation.*

D'Amato, Paul. *The Meaning of Marxism.*

Desmond, Matthew. *Evicted: Poverty and Profit in the American City.*

Engels, Friedrich. *The Principles of Communism.*

Eagleton, Terry. *Why Marx Was Right.*

Gutiérrez, Gustavo. *A Theology of Liberation.*

— *On Job: God-Talk and the Suffering of the Innocent.*

—*On the Side of the Poor: The Theology of Liberation.*

—*The Power Of The Poor In History.*

Harvey, David. *A Brief History of Neoliberalism.*

—*A Companion to Marx's Capital.*

Herzog, Frederick. *Liberation theology: Liberation in the light of the fourth Gospel.*

Heschel, Abraham Joshua. *The Prophets.*

Hunsinger, George. *How to Read Karl Barth.*

—*Karl Barth and Radical Politics, Second Edition.*

— *Thy Word is Truth: Barth on Scripture*

Katch, Danny. *Socialism… Seriously: A Brief Guide to Human Liberation.*

Klein, Naomi. *The Shock Doctrine: The Rise of Disaster Capitalism.*

Lenin, Vladimir. *Imperialism, the Highest Stage of Capitalism.*

Luxemburg, Rosa. *Reform or Revolution and Other Writings.*

Marx, Karl. *Capital.*

—*Grundrisse: Foundations of the Critique of Political Economy.*

—*The German Ideology*

—*Wage Labour and Capital.*

Marx, Karl; Friedrich Engels. *The Communist Manifesto.*

McCormack, Bruce. *Karl Barth's Critically Realistic Dialectical Theology: Its Genesis and Development 1909-1936.*

McMaken, W. Travis. *Our God Loves Justice: An Introduction to Helmut Gollwitzer.*

Moltmann, Jürgen. *Jesus Christ for Today's World.*

— *The Crucified God.*

—*Theology of Hope.*

—*The Spirit of Hope.*

—*The Way of Jesus Christ.*

—*Religion, Revolution, and the Future.*

Miranda, José. *Communism in the Bible.*

—*Marx and the Bible.*

Niebuhr, H. Richard. *Christ and Culture.*

Segundo, S.J., Juan Luis. *The Liberation of Theology.*

Soelle, Dorothee. *Against the Wind: Memoir of a Radical Christian.*

—*On Earth as in Heaven: A Liberation Spirituality of Sharing.*

—*The Strength of the Weak: Toward a Christian Feminist Identity.*

—*Thinking About God: An Introduction to Theology.*

Taylor, Mark Lewis. *The Executed God: The Way of the Cross in Lockdown America.*

Tillich, Paul. *The Socialist Decision.*

—*Systematic Theology.*

Vitale, Alex S. *The End of Policing.*

Weber, Max. *The Protestant Ethic and the "Spirit" of Capitalism.*

Williams, Reggie L. *Bonhoeffer's Black Jesus: Harlem Renaissance Theology and an Ethic of Resistance.*

Wink, Walter. *Jesus and Nonviolence: A Third Way.*

Wiesel, Elie. *Night.*

Woolf, Virginia. *A Room of One's Own.*

Wright, N. T. *Surprised by Hope: Rethinking Heaven, the Resurrection, and the Mission of the Church.*

Yoder, John Howard. *The Politics of Jesus.*

Zinn, Howard. *A People's History of the United States.*

NOTES

Introduction

1. Karl Adams famously called Barth's book "the bomb that fell on the playground of the theologians." For the impact of this text, see Dreyer's essay: http://www.scielo.org.za/scielo.php?script=sci_arttext&pid=S1017-04992017000300008#:~:text=The%20existential%20crisis%20of%20the,Europe%20was%20laid%20to%20ruin. Accessed August 20, 2020.
2. *Liberation Theology: Liberation in the Light of the Fourth Gospel,* viii. New York: The Seabury Press, 1972.
3. https://www.marxists.org/archive/marx/works/1845/theses/index.htm.   Accessed August 20, 2020.
4. Scripture quotations here and throughout are from New Revised Standard Version Bible: Anglicized Edition, copyright © 1989, 1995 National Council of the Churches of Christ in the United States of America. Used by permission. All rights reserved worldwide.
5. See Kendi: *How to Be An Antiracist.*
6. Malcolm X was once approached by a young white woman who asked what she could do to help in the black struggle for liberation. He responded that there was nothing she could do. But later, he came to realize that was a mistake. There is something white people can do: speak out to their fellow whites in their own communities. Instead of trying to "prove" to black people that they are "on their side," Malcolm X writes: "Where the really sincere white people have got to do their proving of themselves is not among the black victims, but on the battle lines of where America's racism really is—and that's in their own home communities; America's racism is among their own fellow whites. That's where the sincere whites who really mean to accomplish something have got to work." *The Autobiography of Malcolm X,* 433. New York: Random House Publishing, 2015.
7. *Black Power,* 4-5; italics original. New York: Vintage Books/Random House, 1967.
8. According to Michelle Alexander: "Studies show that people of all colors *use and sell* illegal drugs at remarkably similar rates." If anything, studies show white teens are *more* likely than their black peers to engage in drug related crimes. See the studies cited in *The New Jim Crow,* 7n10-11. New York: The New Press, 2010.
9. See the studies cited ibid., 207n67.
10. See Kendi: *Stamped From the Beginning.*
11. *Said I Wasn't Gonna Tell Nobody,* 30. New York: Orbis Books, 2018.
12. Peggy McIntosh helpfully lists 50 daily effects of white privilege in her essay, "White Privilege: Unpacking the Invisible Knapsack." These are a good place to start for understanding white privilege, though the list is in no way exhaustive.
13. http://www.sentencingproject.org/publications/color-of-justice-racial-and-ethnic-disparity-in-state-prisons/. Accessed August 20, 2020.
14. See: https://www.theguardian.com/world/2016/oct/04/black-students-teachers-implicit-racial-bias-preschool-study. Accessed July 24, 2020.
15. For this, consider the well-documented sociological theory known as the Pygmalion effect.

Biography

1. *Said I Wasn't Gonna Tell Nobody,* 1. New York: Orbis Books, 2018.
2. *Said I Wasn't Gonna Tell Nobody,* 35. New York: Orbis Books, 2018.
3. *My Soul Looks Back,* 22. New York: Orbis Books, 1986.
4. Ibid., 23.
5. Ibid., 26. I have edited from this quotation a word that I am uncomfortable reprinting, even though it is present in Cone's initial account.
6. Ibid.
7. Ibid., 29.
8. Ibid., 27.
9. Ibid., 34.
10. Ibid.
11. Ibid., 36.
12. Ibid., 37.
13. See *Bonhoeffer's Black Jesus* by Reggie L. Williams.
14. *My Soul Looks Back*, 38-9. New York: Orbis Books, 1986.
15. Ibid., 43.
16. *Said I Wasn't Gonna Tell Nobody,* 1. New York: Orbis Books, 2018.
17. Ibid.
18. *My Soul Looks Back,* 44. New York: Orbis Books, 1986.
19. Ibid., 45.
20. *Said I Wasn't Gonna Tell Nobody,* 2. New York: Orbis Books, 2018.
21. *My Soul Looks Back,* 44. New York: Orbis Books, 1986.
22. *Said I Wasn't Gonna Tell Nobody,* 8. New York: Orbis Books, 2018.
23. Ibid.
24. Ibid., 19.
25. Ibid., 36.
26. *My Soul Looks Back,* 47. New York: Orbis Books, 1986.
27. *Said I Wasn't Gonna Tell Nobody,* 37. New York: Orbis Books, 2018.
28. Ibid.
29. Ibid., 75.
30. *My Soul Looks Back,* 61. New York: Orbis Books, 1986.
31. Ibid., 83.
32. Yale Divinity School, April 2017: "The Cry of Black Blood." https://www.youtube.com/watch?v=kyP7BrmII9U&t=619s. Accessed June 17, 2020.
33. *Said I Wasn't Gonna Tell Nobody,* 92. New York: Orbis Books, 2018.
34. *My Soul Looks Back*, 49. New York: Orbis Books, 1986.
35. *Said I Wasn't Gonna Tell Nobody,* 18. New York: Orbis Books, 2018.
36. Ibid., 61.
37. Ibid., 66.
38. Ibid.
39. Ibid., 81.
40. Ibid., 65.
41. *My Soul Looks Back,* 77. New York: Orbis Books, 1986.
42. Ibid., 77-8.
43. Ibid., 78.
44. Ibid., 57.
45. Ibid.
46. Ibid.
47. *My Soul Looks Back,* 62. New York: Orbis Books, 1986.
48. Ibid., 63.

49. *God of the Oppressed,* 175. New York: The Seabury Press, 1972. The influence of Jürgen Moltmann is apparent. Cone was also fond of Gustavo Gutiérrez's book, *On Job.*
50. *My Soul Looks Back,* 99. New York: Orbis Books, 1986.
51. Ibid., 111.
52. *Said I Wasn't Gonna Tell Nobody,* 108. New York: Orbis Books, 2018.
53. Ibid., 109.
54. *Black Faith and Public Talk,* 252. New York: Orbis Books, 1999.
55. *Said I Wasn't Gonna Tell Nobody,* 110. New York: Orbis Books, 2018.
56. Ibid., 112.
57. Ibid., 171.

1. Black Theology and White Theology

1. Yale Divinity School, April 2017: "The Cry of Black Blood." https://www.youtube.com/watch?v=kyP7BrmII9U&t=619s. Accessed June 17, 2020.
2. *A Black Theology of Liberation,* 1; italics edited for clarity. New York: Orbis Books, 1990.
3. *Black Theology and Ideology,* 44. Collegeville: The Liturgical Press, 2002.
4. *The World Come of Age,* 260. New York: Oxford University Press, 2018.
5. It is worth clarifying here that race is a social construct, not a biological reality. There is only one race, the human race. But because of our social paradigms, it is necessary to speak of black and white races, even if it is not factually accurate, only sociologically relevant.
6. *A Black Theology of Liberation,* xi. New York: Orbis Books, 1990.
7. *The Church and the Power of the Spirit,* 17. Minneapolis: Fortress Press, 1978.
8. https://datacenter.kidscount.org/data/tables/44-children-in-poverty-by-race-and-ethnicity#detailed/1/any/false/37,871,870,573,869,36,868,867,133,38/10,11,9,12,1,185,13/324,323. Accessed June 21, 2020.
9. https://www.sentencingproject.org/wp-content/uploads/2015/12/Race-and-Justice-Shadow-Report-ICCPR.pdf. Accessed June 21, 2020. The actual data is harder to verify, so it could be more or less than 1-3; see this explanation: https://www.washingtonpost.com/news/fact-checker/wp/2015/06/16/the-stale-statistic-that-one-in-three-black-males-has-a-chance-of-ending-up-in-jail/. Access June 21, 2020.
10. Broken window policing is a major reason for the disparity, but that is only part of a much larger issue. Poverty produces crime, and black ghettos are routinely targeted by police as high-crime areas. However, when controlled for socio-economic factors, white people are just as likely to be criminals. The systemic factors of poverty, racism, and incarceration must be factored into our understanding of policing. These statistics are broken down at length in Michele Alexander's *The New Jim Crow,* and *The Color of Law* by Richard Rothstein.
11. https://mappingpoliceviolence.org. Accessed June 21, 2020.
12. According to Nixon's Domestic Affairs Advisor, John Ehrlichman: "We knew we couldn't make it illegal to be either against the war or black, but by getting the public to associate the hippies with marijuana and blacks with heroin, and then criminalizing both heavily, we could disrupt those communities. We could arrest their leaders, raid their homes, break up their meetings, and vilify them night after night on the evening news. Did we know we were lying about the drugs? Of course we did." Interview with Dan Baum for Harper's Magazine April 6, 2016.
13. https://www.theatlantic.com/politics/archive/2018/02/the-trump-administration-finds-that-environmental-racism-is-real/554315/. Accessed June 21, 2020.

14. *God of the Oppressed,* 52. New York: The Seabury Press, 1975.
15. *Black Theology and Ideology,* 19. Collegeville: The Liturgical Press, 2002.
16. Yale Divinity School, April 2017: "The Cry of Black Blood." https://www.youtube.com/watch?v=kyP7BrmII9U&t=619s. Accessed June 17, 2020.
17. *Speaking the Truth,* 39. Grand Rapids: Wm. B. Eerdmans Publishing Co., 1986.
18. *A Black Theology of Liberation,* 45. New York: Orbis Books, 1990.
19. *God of the Oppressed,* 45. New York: The Seabury Press, 1975.
20. See *Church Dogmatics* I/2 §19-21. See also Hunsinger: *Thy Word is Truth: Barth on Scripture.*
21. *A Black Theology of Liberation,* 31. New York: Orbis Books, 1990.
22. Ibid.
23. Ibid.
24. There remain important differences, but I make this comparison to highlight the validity of a community's witness to divine revelation as a source of theology. Barth's concept of preaching does not exactly correspond with Cone's use of the black experience, but their basis is similar enough to be instructive for our purposes. For Barth, see *Church Dogmatics* I/2.
25. *God of the Oppressed,* 33. New York: The Seabury Press, 1975.
26. *Reality and Evangelical Theology,* 17. Philadelphia: The Westminster Press, 1982.
27. *How to Read Karl Barth,* 30. New York: Oxford University Press, 1993.
28. *Black Theology: A Documentary History, 1966-1979,* 101. New York: Orbis Press, 1979.
29. *James H. Cone and Black Liberation Theology,* 119. Jefferson: McFarland & Company, 1994.
30. *A Black Theology of Liberation,* 7n4. New York: Orbis Books, 1990. See also footnote 5.
31. Ibid.
32. Cited in Burrow, 125n49. Jefferson: McFarland & Company, 1994.

2. God is Black

1. *A Black Theology of Liberation,* 63. New York: Orbis Books, 1990.
2. *Risks of Faith,* 32. Boston: Beacon Press, 1999.
3. *God of the Oppressed,* 71. New York: The Seabury Press, 1975.
4. *Cambridge Companion to Black Theology,* 84. Cambridge University Press, 2012.
5. *Systematic Theology Vol. 1,* 63. New York: Oxford University Press, 1997.
6. *Martin & Malcolm & America,* 160. New York: Orbis Books, 1991.
7. See an interesting study done by the University of North Carolina Chapel Hill, the findings of which were summarized here: https://www.vox.com/science-and-health/2018/6/15/17455756/face-of-god-study-plosone-psychology-religion. Accessed June 3, 2020.
8. *God of the Oppressed,* 65. New York: The Seabury Press, 1975.
9. *For My People,* 65. New York: Orbis Books, 1984.
10. *The Spirituals and the Blues,* 102. New York: The Seabury Press, 1972.
11. *Black Theology: A Documentary History, 1966-1979,* 467. New York: Orbis Books, 1979.
12. Cone has Paul Tillich's understanding of "symbol" in mind with this. Tillich distinguishes between a sign and a symbol. The former does not participate in the reality it points to, while the latter does. See Tillich *Dynamics of Faith,* chapter 3, "Symbols of Faith."
13. *Black Theology and Ideology,* 71. Collegeville: The Liturgical Press, 2002.

14. Yale Divinity School, April 2017: "The Cry of Black Blood." https://www.youtube.com/watch?v=kyP7BrmII9U&t=619s. Accessed June 17, 2020.
15. *Are Prisons Obsolete?*, 84. New York: Seven Stories Press, 2003.
16. *Slavery by Another Name.*
17. The amendment reads: "Neither slavery nor involuntary servitude, *except as a punishment for crime* whereof the party shall have been duly convicted, shall exist within the United States, or any place subject to their jurisdiction." Emphasis added.
18. *Freedom Is a Constant Struggle*, 59. Chicago: Haymarket Books, 2015.
19. I cited the statistics and sources for this claim in chapter one, many of which come from Alexander's book *The New Jim Crow*, but it is a well-documented phenomenon I will not rehash here. See the books in Further Reading.
20. *Are Prisons Obsolete?*, 16. New York: Seven Stories Press, 2003.
21. See Angela Davis' work on this subject, *Are Prisons Obsolete?*, which indirectly explains why Christians should fight for prison abolition. I should note here that, as far as I know, James Cone never explicitly endorsed prison abolition. These comments are my contribution, used here to make a point about how white theology aligns itself uncritically with unjust systems of power.
22. We will return to the issue of capitalism in chapter 5.
23. *Martin & Malcolm & America*, 309. New York: Orbis Books, 1991.
24. Interview in *Playboy Magazine*; January, 1965.
25. *A Black Theology of Liberation*, 72-3. New York: Orbis Books, 1990.

3. The Gospel of Liberation

1. *Black Theology and Black Power*, 38. New York: The Seabury Press, 1969.
2. *Said I Wasn't Gonna Tell Nobody*, 140. New York: Orbis Books: 2018.
3. *Strength to Love*, 131-2. Philadelphia: Fortress Press, 1981.
4. *A Theology of Liberation*, 115. New York: Orbis Books, 1973.
5. *Black Theology: A Documentary History, 1966-1979*, 499. New York: Orbis Books, 1979.
6. Luke 4:18-19.
7. *God of the Oppressed*, 135. New York: The Seabury Press, 1975.
8. Ibid., 134.
9. Ibid., 137.
10. *Speaking the Truth*, 37. Grand Rapids: Wm. B. Eermans, 1986.
11. In lieu of a more precise argument against escapism, I recommend N. T. Wright's *Surprised by Hope* and Moltmann's *Theology of Hope*. In short, Moltmann said it best: "I don't want to go to heaven. Heaven is there for the angels, and I am a child of the earth. But I expect passionately the world to come: The new heaven and the new earth where justice dwells, where God will wipe away every tear and make all things new. And this expectation makes life in this world for me, here and now, most lovable." https://www.youtube.com/watch?v=yUY2T8KaFgk. Accessed August 20, 2020.
12. *Theology of Hope*, 21. Philadelphia: Fortress Press, 1964.
13. *A Black Theology of Liberation*, 137. New York: Orbis Books, 1990.
14. *Black Theology: A Documentary History, 1966-1979*, 539. New York: Orbis Books, 1979.
15. Ibid., 392.
16. Yale Divinity School, April 2017: "The Cry of Black Blood." https://www.youtube.com/watch?v=kyP7BrmII9U&t=619s. Accessed June 17, 2020.
17. *Black Theology: A Documentary History, 1966-1979*, 540-1. New York: Orbis Books, 1979.

18. https://www.africa.upenn.edu/Articles_Gen/Letter_Birmingham.html. Accessed June 25, 2020.
19. *A Black Theology of Liberation*, 140. New York: Orbis Books, 1990.
20. *God of the Oppressed*, 78. New York: The Seabury Press, 1975.
21. *The Fire Next Time*, 83. New York: Dial Press, 1963.
22. *Black Theology and Black Power*, 41. New York: The Seabury Press, 1969.
23. *The Spirit of Hope*, 10. Louisville: Westminster John Knox Press, 2019.
24. *The Cross and the Lynching Tree*, 158. New York: Orbis Books, 2011.
25. Ibid., xv.
26. Ibid., 161.
27. *Letters and Papers from Prison*. DBW, Vol. 8, 479. Minneapolis: Fortress Press, 2010.
28. *The Cross and the Lynching Tree*, 160. New York: Orbis Books, 2011.
29. Ibid., 165.

4. Becoming Black with Christ

1. *Black Theology and Black Power*, 67. New York: The Seabury Press, 1969.
2. *A Black Theology of Liberation*, 88. New York: Orbis Books, 1990.
3. *A Theology of Liberation*, xxxi. New York: Orbis Books, 1973.
4. *James H. Cone and Black Liberation Theology*, 46. Jefferson: McFarland & Company, 1994.
5. *Black Theology and Black Power*, 150. New York: The Seabury Press, 1969.
6. Ibid., 151.
7. *Discipleship*, 87n11 (DBW, Vol. 4). According to the translators, this popular aphorism is not quite accurate. The German is more faithfully rendered, "Whenever Christ calls us, his call leads us to death." But I quote the famous aphorism here because it is the one Cone used to conclude his first essay, "Christianity and Black Power" (1968).
8. *A Black Theology of Liberation*, 66. New York: Orbis Books, 1990.
9. *The Cambridge Companion to Black Theology*, 149. Cambridge University Press: 2012.
10. *Black Theology and Black Power*, 152. New York: The Seabury Press, 1969.
11. *A Black Theology of Liberation*, 7. New York: Orbis Books, 1990.
12. Leonardo and Clodovis Boff explain the problem with charity: "There is a failure to see that the poor are oppressed and made poor *by others;* and what they do possess— strength to resist, capacity to understand their rights, to organize themselves and transform a subhuman situation—tends to be left out of account. Aid [i.e., charity] increases the dependence of the poor, tying them to help from others, to decisions made by others: again, not enabling them to become their own liberators." *Introducing Liberation Theology*, 4. New York: Orbis Books, 1987.
13. *For My People*, 197. New York: Orbis Books, 1984.
14. *Helder, the Gift*, 53. Editora Vozes, 2000.
15. *Introducing Liberation Theology*, 7. New York: Orbis Books, 1987.
16. *Black Theology and Black Power*, 15. New York: The Seabury Press, 1969.
17. *Black Power*, 47. New York: Vintage Books/Random House, 1967.
18. *Communities of Resistance: Writings on Black Struggles for Socialism*, 99. New York: Verso, 1990.
19. *Black Theology and Black Power*, 2. New York: The Seabury Press, 1969.
20. *A Black Theology of Liberation*, 108. New York: Orbis Books, 1990.
21. *Christian Faith*, 428. Louisville: Westminster John Knox Press, 2016.
22. Ibid, 483.
23. *Suffering*, 157. Philadelphia: Fortress Press, 1975.
24. *A Black Theology of Liberation*, 94-5, 101. New York: Orbis Books, 1990.

5. The Ethics of Liberation

1. *For My People,* 118. New York: Orbis Books, 1984.
2. *My Soul Looks Back,* 106-7. New York: Orbis: 1986.
3. *The Black Church and Marxism,* 5. New York: The Institute for Democratic Socialism, 1980.
4. *Against the Wind,* 47-8. Minneapolis: Fortress Press, 1999.
5. *Said I Wasn't Gonna Tell Nobody,* 116. New York: Orbis Books, 2018.
6. *God of the Oppressed,* 218. New York: The Seabury Press, 1975.
7. Ibid.
8. Ibid., 219.
9. *Requiem for a Nun,* 85. London: Chatto & Windus, 1919.
10. *Black Theology and Black Power,* 143. New York: The Seabury Press, 1969.
11. Of course, no one wants violence. The goal is not violence but justice. I do not mean to imply here that violence is inevitable, but when we soberly assess the present reality of political and social marginalization, it is highly unlikely that the revolution will be non-violent. Those in power, the oppressors of the poor and black, have made it nearly impossible to achieve justice non-violently by systemically excluding non-violent pathways to a better world. As Christians, we hope and pray for non-violent solutions, but we also must be realists. And we must always remember who fired the first shot: the violence of the oppressors far outweighs that of the oppressed who rise up in revolt against the chains that bind them.
12. *God of the Oppressed,* 217. New York: The Seabury Press, 1975.
13. *Risks of Faith,* 39. Boston: Beacon Press, 1999.
14. *Speaking the Truth,* 123. Grand Rapids: Wm. B. Eerdmans, 1986.
15. https://www.cbsnews.com/news/40-of-americans-one-step-from-poverty-if-they-miss-a-paycheck/ Accessed July 5, 2020.
16. *Black Theology: A Documentary History, 1966-1979,* 356. New York: Orbis Books, 1979.
17. *The Great Economic Debate: An Ethical Analysis,* 55. Philadelphia: Westminster Press, 1977.
18. *The Black Church and Marxism,* 9. New York: The Institute for Democratic Socialism, 1980.
19. *Introducing Liberation Theology,* 28. New York: Orbis Books, 1987.
20. *My Soul Looks Back,* 131. New York: Orbis Books, 1986.
21. Ibid., 107.
22. Ibid.
23. *For My People,* 186. New York: Orbis Books, 1984.
24. For more on the neo-liberal, corporatist project, see Naomi Klein's important book, *The Shock Doctrine.*
25. *My Soul Looks Back,* 107. New York: Orbis Books, 1986.
26. Ibid.
27. *The Black Church and Marxism,* 10. New York: The Institute for Democratic Socialism, 1980.
28. *Introducing Liberation Theology,* 60. New York: Orbis Books, 1987.
29. *A Black Theology of Liberation,* xv. New York: Orbis Books, 1990.
30. *Black Theology: A Documentary History, 1966-1979,* 377. New York: Orbis Books, 1979.
31. Although the rate has been steadily declining since its peak in 2000, black women still have the highest imprisonment rate of any other group. The war on drugs is a primary reason for this. https://www.sentencingproject.org/publications/incarcerated-women-and-girls/. Accessed July 2, 2020.

32. https://www.nj.com/news/2020/07/trading-sex-for-toilet-paper-and-bubble-gum-inmates-detail-abuse-by-guards-in-njs-womens-prison.html. Accessed July 3, 2020.
33. See "How Gender Structures the Prison System" in Angela Davis' book *Are Prisons Obsolete?*
34. Matthew Desmond: https://www.macfound.org/media/files/HHM_Research_Brief_-_Poor_Black_Women_Are_Evicted_at_Alarming_Rates.pdf. Accessed July 1, 2020. Also see Desmond's book, *Evicted.*
35. https://www.nbcnews.com/health/womens-health/u-s-finally-has-better-maternal-mortality-data-black-mothers-n1125896. Accessed July 1, 2020.

Conclusion

1. *The Prophets,* 5. New York: Harper & Row Publishers, 1962.
2. Ibid., 26.
3. Ibid., 5.
4. Ibid., 10.
5. *Speaking the Truth,* 57. Grand Rapids: Wm. B. Eerdmans, 1986.
6. *Black Theology and Black Power,* 2. New York: The Seabury Press, 1969.

ALSO BY STEPHEN D. MORRISON

Plain English Series:

Karl Barth in Plain English (2017)

T. F. Torrance in Plain English (2017)

Jürgen Moltmann in Plain English (2018)

Schleiermacher in Plain English (2019)

James Cone in Plain English (2020)

Selected bibliography:

Welcome Home: The Good News of Jesus (2016)

10 Reasons Why the Rapture Must be Left Behind (2015)

We Belong: Trinitarian Good News (2015)

For a full list of titles, visit:

www.SDMorrison.org

Made in the USA
Columbia, SC
09 December 2020

27186623R00075